Barron's Book Notes

A Simplified Approach to

Emily Dickinson

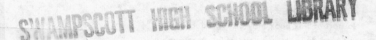

By **ROBERT L. LAIR**
Professor of English
Malone College
Canton, Ohio

Barron's Educational Series, Inc.

Woodbury, New York

All inquiries should be addressed to:

BARRON'S EDUCATIONAL SERIES, INC.
113 Crossways Park Drive
Woodbury, New York 11797

Library of Congress Catalog Card No. 72-108022

International Standard Book No. 0-8120-0398-5

Printed in the United States of America

TO ZOVINAR

Nor had I time to love. But since
Some industry must be—
The little toil of love, I thought,
Be large enough for me.
(#478)

Acknowledgments

The analysis of Emily Dickinson's "As by the dead we love to sit" first appeared in *The Explicator* (March 1967) and is here reprinted by permission.

The numbers and dates given for individual lyrics are those assigned them by Thomas H. Johnson in *The Poems of Emily Dickinson* (Cambridge, Massachusetts: The Belknap Press of Harvard University Press, 1955) and are used by permission.

Contents

Chronology

LIFE	WORK

1830   December 10—Emily Dickinson born to Emily Norcross and Edward Dickinson at Amherst, Massachusetts, in the homestead built by her grandfather.

1835   Edward Dickinson made treasurer of Amherst College (remained so until 1872).

1840   The poet attended Amherst Academy (until 1847).

The Dickinsons moved from the family homestead on Main Street to a home on Pleasant Street (remained there until November 1855).

1844   April 29—Sophia Holland, but one year older than Emily Dickinson, died. Her death affected the poet deeply.

1847   Emily Dickinson enrolled in Mt. Holyoke Female Seminary in nearby South Hadley, Massachusetts (though sick with a bronchial ailment for a while and quite unhappy, she stayed the year).

1848-50   Ben Newton, a lawyer's apprentice in her father's office, was her companion.

1850   Her brother, William Austin Dickinson, graduated from Amherst College.

Ben Newton moved to Worcester, Massachusetts.

WORK: "Awake Ye Muses Nine" was published in the Amherst College *Indicator*.

1851   Samuel Bowles, a close friend of the Dickinson family, succeeded his father as editor of the *Springfield Daily Republican* (a number of Emily Dickinson's poems were first published here).

       Ben Newton married.

1852   Edward Dickinson went to Congress as a Whig Republican.

1853   Edward Dickinson made a representative to Congress (until 1855).

       March 24—Ben Newton died of consumption (aged 33).

1854   William Austin Dickinson admitted to the bar; practiced law in Amherst.

1855   April—Edward Dickinson bought back the family homestead on Main Street in Amherst.

       October—the family moved into the house.

       Emily and her sister made a trip to Washington where her father was finishing his term as a representative to the Congress. They stopped in Philadelphia where they met Rev. Charles Wadsworth, Emily's spiritual adviser who helped her through a difficult emotional period and with whom she seems to have fallen in love.

1856   July 1—Susan Gilbert married Emily's brother Austin. The newlyweds lived next door to Emily Dickinson in a house their father built. Sue was the recipient of many of Emily's lyrics.

       October—Emily Dickinson won second prize at a cattle show for her rye and Indian bread.

February 20—"A Valentine: Sic Transit Gloria Mundi" was published in the *Springfield Daily Republican.*

1857   Ralph Waldo Emerson, lecturing
        in Amherst, visited in her broth-
        er's home.

1858   She began to tie together her
        poems into small bundles, pos-
        sibly with a view to later publica-
        tion.

1859   The morns are meeker than they were
                                                    (12)*
                                                Heart! We will forget him! (47)
                                                I never lost as much but twice (49)

                                                A little east of Jordan (59)
                                                Papa above! (61)
                                                Success is counted sweetest (67)
                                                Exultation is the going (76)
                                                As by the dead we love to sit (88)
                                                One dignity delays for all (98)
                                                To fight aloud is very brave (126)
                                                These are the days when birds come back
                                                    (130)
                                                An altered look about the hills (140)

1860   Rev. Charles Wadsworth visited   Dust is the only secret (153)
        her at Amherst.   Just lost, when I was saved! (160)
                                                A wounded deer leaps highest (165)
                                                If I shouldn't be alive (182)
                                                Faith is a fine invention (185)
                                                I shall know why when time is over (193)
                                                I'm wife—I've finished that (199)
                                                Come slowly, Eden (211)
                                                I taste a liquor never brewed (214)
                                                Some keep the sabbath going to church
                                                    (324)

1861   June — her nephew, Edward   May 4—"The May Wine: I Taste a Liquor
        ("Ned") Dickinson, Austin and   Never Brewed" was published in the
        Sue's first son, born.   Springfield Daily Republican.
                                                Safe in their alabaster chambers (216)
                                                Savior! I've no one else to tell (217)
                                                The lamp burns sure within (233)
                                                I like a look of agony (241)
                                                I've known a heaven, like a tent (243)
                                                I can wade grief (252)

---

* Unless otherwise noted, poems are assigned to probable year of writing as arranged by Thomas H. Johnson, *The Poems of Emily Dickinson*, three volumes, Cambridge: Harvard University Press, 1955.

Hope is the thing with feathers (254)
Delight is as the flight (257)
There's a certain slant of light (258)
I felt a funeral in my brain (280)
'Tis so appalling it exhilarates (281)
The robin's my criterion for tune (285)
A clock stopped (287)
I'm nobody! Who are you? (288)
I know some lonely houses off the road (289)
I got so I could take his name (293)
There came a day at summer's full (322)
Of tribulation, these are they (325)

1862 April 15—the poet wrote to Thomas Wentworth Higginson (editor of *Atlantic Monthly*) to ask his estimate of her poetry (she sent him four lyrics). The correspondence continued until her death.

She was suffering some emotional crisis. Began to dress in white. Upset over Wadsworth's leaving.

She wrote more poetry than in any other year. A great creative burst of energy.

May 1—Wadsworth left Arch Street Presbyterian Church in Philadelphia to assume the pastorate of Calvary Church in San Francisco.

March 1—"The Sleeping: Safe in Their Alabaster Chambers" was published in the *Springfield Daily Republican*.
Your riches taught me poverty (299)
I reason, earth is short (301)
The soul selects her own society (303)
The difference between despair (305)
The soul's superior instants (306)
He fumbles at your soul (315)
I'll tell you how the sun rose (318)
Of all the sounds despatched abroad (321)
I cannot dance upon my toes (326)
Before I got my eye put out (327)
A bird came down the walk (328)
The grass so little has to do (333)
I know that He exists (338)
After great pain, a formal feeling comes (341)
I dreaded that first robin so (348)
I felt my life with both my hands (351)
God is a distant stately Lover (357)
Death sets a thing significant (360)
Dare you see a soul at the white heat? (365)
She lay as if at play (369)
I'm saying every day (373)
Of course I prayed (376)
Exhilaration is within (383)
No rack can torture me (384)
There's been a death in the opposite house (389)
What soft cherubic creatures (401)
They dropped like flakes (409)
The first day's night had come (410)
The color of the grave is green (411)
I read my sentence steadily (412)
I never felt at home below (413)

1864   February and April—the poet
        made trips to Boston for treatment
        of an eye affliction.

March 12—"My Sabbath: Some Keep the
    Sabbath Going to Church" was pub-
    lished in *The Round Table*.
March 30—"Sunset: Blazing In Gold and
    Quenching In Purple" was published in
    the *Springfield Daily Republican*.
Ample make this bed (829)
There is a finished feeling (856)
Split the lark and you'll find the music
    (861)
Till death is narrow loving (907)
The heart has narrow banks (928)
Unto Me? I do not know you (964)
Death is a dialogue between (976)

1865   The poet made further trips to
        Boston for eye treatment; ap-
        parently she was finally cured.

        She seems never to have left
        Amherst again.

A narrow fellow in the grass (986)
Crumbling is not an instant's act (997)
Bind me—I still can sing (1005)
I never saw a moor (1052)
As imperceptibly as grief (1540)

1866   November 30—Her niece, Martha
        Gilbert Dickinson born to Austin
        and Sue.

February 14—"The Snake: A Narrow Fel-
    low in the Grass" was published in the
    Springfield Daily Republican.
Further in summer than the birds (1068)
The bustle in a house (1078)
Revolution is the pod (1082)
At half past three, a single bird (1084)
The last night that she lived (1100)

1869

After a hundred years (1147)

1870   August 17—Thomas Wentworth
        Higginson visited the poet at
        Amherst.

        Rev. Charles Wadsworth returned
        from California to Philadelphia.

We never know how high we are (1176)

1872

He preached upon "Breadth" till it argued
    him narrow (1207)

1873   December 3—Thomas Wentworth
        Higginson visited the poet a sec-
        ond time.

A word dropped careless on a page (1261)
There is no frigate like a book (1263)

1874   June 16—Edward Dickinson died
        of apoplexy in Boston (attending
        a legislative session of the Gen-
        eral Court of Massachusetts).

1875	June 15—The poet's mother suffered a paralytic stroke which left her an invalid for her remaining years.	
	August 1—Her nephew, Thomas Gilbert ("Gib") Dickinson, born to Austin and Sue.	
1876	August 20—Helen Hunt Jackson (an acclaimed poet of her day) asked Emily Dickinson for a poetic contribution to *A Masque of Poets*.	The rat is the concisest tenant (1356) The bat is dun with wrinkled wings (1575)
1877	Her dear friend Judge Otis Lord's wife died.	
1878	Her friend and correspondent Samuel Bowles died.	November—"Success: Success Is Counted Sweetest" was published in *A Masque of Poets*, edited by Helen Hunt Jackson.
1879		A route of evanescence (1463)
1880	Summer—Rev. Charles Wadsworth visited Emily Dickinson a second time.	
1881		How happy is the little stone (1510)
1882	April—Rev. Charles Wadsworth died.	The Bible is an antique volume (1545) Elysium is as far as to (1760)
	November 14—Her mother, Emily Norcross Dickinson, died.	
1883	October 5 — Her eight-year-old nephew, Thomas Gilbert Dickinson, died suddenly of typhoid fever.	
1884	March—Judge Otis Lord died.	Apparently with no surprise (1624)
	June 14—The poet suffered a nervous breakdown.	
1885	August 12—Helen Hunt Jackson died.	
	November—from this point the poet was confined to her bed and room (suffering from nephritis).	

1886   May 15—The poet died at Am-
        herst.

Undated poems discussed here: Death is like the insect (1716)
                                         My life closed twice before its close (1732)

*   *   *   *   *

POSTHUMOUS PUBLICATIONS

1890 *Poems by Emily Dickinson* (ed. Mabel Loomis Todd and Thomas Wentworth
     Higginson)

1891 *Poems by Emily Dickinson: Second Series* (ed. Mabel Loomis Todd and Thomas
     Wentworth Higginson)

1894 *The Letters of Emily Dickinson,* two volumes (ed. Mabel Loomis Todd)

1896 *Poems by Emily Dickinson: Third Series* (ed. Mabel Loomis Todd)

1914 *The Single Hound: Poems of a Lifetime* (ed. Martha Dickinson Bianchi)

1924 *The Life and Letters of Emily Dickinson* (ed. Martha Dickinson Bianchi)

     The Complete Poems of Emily Dickinson (ed. Martha Dickinson Bianchi and Alfred
     Leete Mampson)

1929 *Further Poems of Emily Dickinson Withheld from Publication by Her Sister Lavinia*
     (ed. Martha Dickinson Bianchi)

1931 *Letters of Emily Dickinson* (ed. Mabel Loomis Todd)

1932 *Emily Dickinson Face to Face: Unpublished Letters with Notes and Reminiscences*
     (ed. Martha Dickinson Bianchi)

1935 *Unpublished Poems of Emily Dickinson* (ed. Martha Dickinson Bianchi and Alfred
     Leete Hampson)

1937 *Poems by Emily Dickinson* (ed. Martha Dickinson Bianchi and Alfred Leete Hamp-
     son)

1945 *Bolts of Melody: New Poems by Emily Dickinson* (ed. Mabel Loomis Todd and
     Millicent Todd Bingham)

1951 *Emily Dickinson's Letters to Dr. and Mrs. Josiah Gilbert Holland* (ed. Theodora
     Van Wagenen Ward)

1955 *The Poems of Emily Dickinson,* three volumes (The definitive edition upon which
     all subsequent texts must be based. Ed. Thomas H. Johnson)

1958 *The Letters of Emily Dickinson,* three volumes (The definitive edition upon which
     all subsequent texts must be based. Ed. Thomas H. Johnson and Theodora Van
     Wagenen Ward)

Biographical Sketch

When Thomas Wentworth Higginson, the nineteenth-century Unitarian clergyman and editor of *Atlantic Monthly,* asked Emily Dickinson for some description of her life and activities, she answered each of his questions cryptically:

You asked how old I was? I made no verse, but one or two until this winter, sir.

I had a terror since September, I could tell to none; and so I sing, as the boy does by the burying ground, because I am afraid.

You inquire my books. For poets, I have Keats, and Mr. and Mrs. Browning. For prose, Mr. Ruskin, Sir Thomas Browne, and the Revelations [sic]. I went to school, but in your manner of the phrase had no education. When a little girl, I had a friend who taught me Immortality; but venturing too near, himself, he never returned. Soon after my tutor died, and for several years my lexicon was my only companion. Then I found one more, but he was not contented I be his scholar, so he left the land.

You ask of my companions. Hills, sir, and the sundown, and a dog large as myself, that my father bought me. They are better than beings, because they know, but do not tell; and the noise in the pool at noon excels my piano.

I have a brother and sister; my mother does not care for thought, and father, too busy with his briefs to notice what we do. He buys me many books, but begs me not to read them, because he fears they joggle the mind.

So intrigued was Higginson by her cryptic response that he asked for her picture. Again her instinctive reticence put him off:

I had no portrait, but am small, like the wren; and my hair is bold like the chestnut bur; and my eyes, like the sherry in the glass, that the guest leaves. Would this do just as well?

Finally, in August of 1870, eight years after his first missive from her, Higginson stopped at Amherst to see his "Gnome." His description of that visit only confirms the impression of oddity which one feels initially about the poet:

> It was at her father's house, one of those large, square, brick mansions so familiar in our older New England towns, surrounded by trees and blossoming shrubs without, and within exquisitely neat, cool, spacious, and fragrant with flowers. After a little delay, I heard an extremely faint and pattering footstep like that of a child, in the hall, and in glided, almost noiselessly, a plain, shy little person, the face without a single good feature, but with eyes, as she herself said "like the sherry the guest leaves in the glass," and with smooth bands of reddish chestnut hair. She had a quaint and nun-like look, as if she might be a German canoness of some religious order, whose prescribed garb was white piqué, with a blue net worsted shawl. She came toward me with two day-lilies, which she put in a childlike way into my hand, saying softly, under her breath, "These are my introduction," and adding, also under her breath, in childlike fashion, "Forgive me if I am frightened; I never see strangers, and hardly know what to say."

Higginson admitted that his interview with Emily Dickinson left him with an impression of "something abnormal."

> She was much too enigmatical a being for me to solve in an hour's interview. . . . I could only sit and watch, as one does in the woods.

The personality of Emily Dickinson seems destined to remain an enigma; her biography is surrounded by the mystery of her shyness (was it the product of some aborted love, or did it manifest itself as a natural part of the woman's temperament?), her inability to engage in the "normal" activities of life, her utter withdrawal from the surrounding neighborhood of her native Amherst.

We do have certain "facts." We know, for example, that she was born on December 10, 1830, at Amherst, Massachusetts (in the Dickinson homestead fashioned by her grandfather), the daughter of Edward and Emily Norcross Dickinson, born in the third year of their marriage, the second of three children (her brother, William Austin, had been born twenty months earlier on April 16, 1829; her sister, Lavinia, was born twenty-six months later on February 28, 1833). She spent seven years (1840-47) at Amherst Academy where she learned, among other things, Latin, French, and German, and where she was aided in her studies by the principal, Leonard Humphrey.

She enrolled in Mt. Holyoke Female Seminary in nearby South

Hadley, Massachusetts, in the fall of 1847, and, though she suffered a severe bronchial illness and was quite unhappy, she finished out the year there. It was in this same year that the young lawyer's apprentice, Ben Newton, came to work in her father's law office. She had referred to him in her letter to Higginson as the "friend who taught me Immortality; but venturing too near, himself, he never returned." (Incidentally, he had moved from Amherst to Wooster, Massachusetts, in 1850, married there in 1851, and died of consumption at thirty-three on March 24, 1853.) Ben Newton had been a close companion and an intellectual stimulus to her imagination. His death was shattering to her, and she commemorated it in a number of anniversary lyrics.

In 1852, her father went to Congress as a Whig Republican (he was a man active in public life, having served as well in the state legislature and as treasurer of Amherst College). Two years later, Emily and Lavinia went to Washington to meet their father when he finished his term as representative. It was on that trip that the poet likely met Rev. Charles Wadsworth, the young clergyman who was to figure prominently in her life, though the exact role he played remains still somewhat mysterious (the correspondence is not extant). It has been conjectured that Wadsworth saw the poet's need for spiritual counsel and gave it, that he admired her poetic gift and praised it, that she took his intimate conversations and letters to her much too seriously, thinking they expressed love for her. It is to Wadsworth that Emily Dickinson refers in her letter to Higginson: "Then I found one more, but he was not contented I be his scholar, so he left the land." Wadsworth visited Emily Dickinson at Amherst in 1860, an event about which there have been a century of rumors. In 1862, he left his pastorate of the Arch Street Presbyterian Church in Philadelphia to assume the duties of the Calvary Church in San Francisco. He returned to Philadelphia in 1870 and, ten years later, in the summer of 1880, visited the poet a second time. Two years after his visit, he was dead. It is thought most of the love lyrics were composed for him; in Untermeyer's phrase, she felt "dedicated" to his "spirit."

In 1856, Emily's brother, William Austin Dickinson, married Susan Gilbert. The newlyweds moved into the house next door to the Dickinsons, into a house their father had built. While Sue was "only a lawn away," Emily rarely visited in their home, sending instead cryptic messages, often with new lyrics penned in them, to her nearest neighbor and sister-in-law (she had posted over three hundred poems in all to her). In that same year, 1856, Emily Dickinson won second prize at the cattle show for her rye and Indian bread. But she rarely left their Amherst dwelling after that, except to make visits to Boston in 1864 and 1865 for treatment of an eye affliction.

In 1862, a difficult year for the poet, she initiated a correspondence with Colonel Thomas Wentworth Higginson, having read some of his poetic reviews in the *Atlantic Monthly*. She had begun to tie her scraps of manuscripts together in 1858, possibly planning to seek publication for them (though she later wrote: "Publication is the auction of the mind of man"). The intellectual stimulation of both Ben Newton and Charles Wadsworth cut off, she sought frantically for a sympathetic ear, a kindred spirit who could set her creative gift in the right direction. Unfortunately, though Higginson was both patient and sympathetic, encouraging the poet earnestly, he had little real comprehension of the genius he was touching. His tastes were toward the more conservative, precisely composed lyrics of the second-rate talents of his day. While we owe him a great debt (particularly for his role in bringing the poet to public attention, both in writing of her and in editing the lyrics with Mrs. Todd), his chief contribution to Emily Dickinson's career lies in his continual encouragement of her labors.

I referred earlier to 1862 as a year of great emotional crisis. It was the year in which Wadsworth was to leave Philadelphia, to take residence in remote California, a severance which Emily Dickinson could not accept without grief. There may too have been some psychic anguish over her having passed the age of thirty, settling more and more surely into spinsterhood, another state which she could not graciously accept (as her lyrics continually attest, her striving again and again to convince us that she is "wife"). She dressed from this year forward in white, as if ready at a moment's notice for that wedding she knew could never be. Nonetheless, this is the year of the poet's greatest creative output. More of the best lyrics are dated in this year than in any other before or after it. Out of her deep emotional distress came some of the most compelling lyrics.

The last fifteen years of Emily Dickinson's life were punctuated by visitations of sorrow. Her father died on June 16, 1874, while attending the legislative session of the General Court of Massachusetts in Boston. A year later, almost to the day, her mother suffered a paralytic stroke which left her an invalid until her death in 1882 (she was throughout her seven remaining years a perpetual burden to Emily and Lavinia). In 1877, a dear friend, Judge Otis Lord, lost his wife (some contend he later proposed marriage to the poet); a year later, her friend and correspondent Samuel Bowles died.

In 1883, one year after her mother's death, Emily Dickinson's nephew Thomas, only eight at the time, died suddenly of typhoid fever. In March of the following year, Judge Lord himself died. By June, the poet had suffered a complete emotional collapse. Confined to her room a little over a year, she died of nephritis on May 15, 1886, at Amherst. On her tombstone is carved the laconic "Called back."

Little noticed by the world in those fifty-six years of her life, Emily Dickinson has become since her death one of the major figures of American poetry, judged by some to be one of the greatest poets of all times. Imagine her sister's surprise when, after Emily's funeral, she opened the now-fabled drawer which contained so many of those seventeen hundred lyrics.

Publication History

Having discovered those bundles of lyrics, Lavinia Dickinson began the task of reading and sorting through them. Having decided they might be suitable for publication, she gained the help of Mabel Loomis Todd and Thomas Wentworth Higginson to prepare them for publication. Together these latter two brought out two volumes of her poems (1890, 1891). Later, Mrs. Todd alone prepared a third volume of the poems (1896) and a two-volume set of the letters (1894).

In 1914, Emily Dickinson's niece, Martha Dickinson Bianchi, prepared the volume *The Single Hound,* a collection of the lyrics. In 1924, she produced *The Life and Letters of Emily Dickinson* and, with Alfred Leete Hampson, *The Complete Poems of Emily Dickinson* (though we now know the collection was by no means complete; in fact, Mrs. Bianchi, in 1929, published *Further Poems of Emily Dickinson Withheld from Publication by Her Sister Lavinia*). Still later, in 1935, she and Hampson brought out another volume, *Unpublished Poems of Emily Dickinson.* And still later, in 1945, Mrs. Todd and her daughter, Millicent Todd Bingham, published *Bolts of Melody: New Poems by Emily Dickinson.* (Note: unfortunately, most of these early texts were tampered with by the editors, making them unsuitable for careful study.)

The letters of Emily Dickinson likewise were so absorbing to the student of her poems that, in addition to the earlier editions of her letters (1894, 1924), Mrs. Todd edited the *Letters of Emily Dickinson* (1931), and Mrs. Bianchi *Emily Dickinson Face to Face: Unpublished Letters with Notes and Reminiscences.* In 1951, Theodora Van Wagenen Ward edited and published *Emily Dickinson's Letters to Dr. and Mrs. Josiah Gilbert Holland.*

It was not until the decade of the fifties, however, that the really important textual work was done on Emily Dickinson's poems and letters. Harvard University had been given most of the Dickinson manuscripts. They were turned over to Thomas H. Johnson who, after careful research and study, edited the definitive text of her lyrics:

The Poems of Emily Dickinson (in three volumes, Harvard University Press, 1955). Three years later, and with the help of Mrs. Ward, Johnson had completed *The Letters of Emily Dickinson*. These are the authoritative texts with all variant readings both from manuscripts and from earlier editions.

General Introduction

Emily Dickinson had no abstract theory of poetry. If she defined it at all in her own mind, her definiton is only implicit in her practice of the art. Whether or not she had read the poetic theories of her predecessors and contemporaries or knew of them is as well an unanswerable question. She lived in an age that had begun to formulate a critical philosophy of poetry, in the century which gave us Poe, Emerson, and Whitman, as well as Coleridge and Matthew Arnold. Yet she seems as oblivious of their pronouncements as she does of the Civil War.

When she did define poetry for Higginson, she could appeal only to her own subjectively emotional response to it:

> If I read a book and it makes my whole body so cold no fire can ever warm me, I know that is poetry. If I feel physically as if the top of my head were taken off, I know that is poetry. These are the only ways I know it. Is there any other way?

Cryptic, enigmatic her definition is. Yet she insisted firmly upon it.

Whatever her own views of poetry, critics have, since her work first appeared, associated her creations with other traditions in British and American literature. The commonest identification of Miss Dickinson's poetry is with that of the Seventeenth-Century Metaphysical Poets. We know that she read a great deal and that she had especially enjoyed the books of the Seventeenth-Century authors, partly because of their religious qualities and partly because of the concreteness of their metaphorical utterances. If we were to compare Miss Dickinson's "I like to see it lap the miles" (585) with, say, the lyrics of John Donne, there would be obvious differences: Donne's lyrics are nearly all either erotic or religious, while this sample of Miss Dickinson's is neither. The nineteenth-century poet has seen the powerful engine of the great new iron horse stepping across an expanding America; she expresses a childlike fascination and imaginative awe which she feels at the sight, but strikingly she effects the entire lyric by elaboration of the metaphor of train and horse. The train prances proudly, neighing like Boanerges, feeding itself at the fuel tanks along the way, until at last it arrives at its own stable door. Here is a metaphor elaborated with all the ingenuity and consistency of, certainly a Herbert, if not a Donne.

There are other critics who speak of the Emersonian quality in the verse of Emily Dickinson. It is true that her frequent voicing of ideas of independence and individualism, of reaction against conformity and obeissance to tradition, provide us a poetic variation upon the theme of self-reliance. There is also the romantic notion of the relationship between beauty and truth which we find in Emerson (perhaps through Keats) and which is reiterated in Miss Dickinson's verse. For Emerson, beauty and virtue were the same thing (here was, in fact, one of the bases of Poe's violent reaction to Emerson; for Poe, the only points at which beauty and virtue touched were those at which vice could be equated with the ugly, since the sole province of art was beauty and never morality). For the Romantic poet (and even for Matthew Arnold later), art would replace religion as the arbiter of morality and virtue. Keats had stated this thought most succinctly at the end of his "Ode on a Grecian Urn." Whether Miss Dickinson's source was Keats or Emerson (I am convinced it was Keats), the motif does cause critics to comment on her Emersonianism. [Note: I refer here to a particular lyric, #449, "I died for beauty," in which Miss Dickinson finds herself settled in the grave next to one who died for truth; the conclusion to which she comes is that their cause was one: to die for beauty is to die for truth; the two are the same.]

A third tradition to which Miss Dickinson has been related is that of the laconic New England poets and writers of fiction, both those who had preceded her and those who would follow her. It is Mr. Whicher's argument, as well as that of other critics, that Emily Dickinson is the product of her own New England environment and way of life. It has been characteristic of New England people, the argument runs, to be shy, withdrawn, to say little, but to convey much. For illustration, the critics draw generally from Hawthorne's concisest fictions and look forward to Robert Frost's later synecdoches. The New England temperament, with its tendency toward conciseness and contraction, toward suggestiveness and understatement, has produced a strain of American writers whose characteristics can be clearly related. Emily Dickinson is a part of that school. An examination of her poetry is certainly convincing: she never writes a long poem (though it may be argued that the reason is that she was interested in the lyric, not in the dramatic or the narrative genres; certainly she had no such critical conviction as Poe's that there was no long poem), but tends toward the epigrammatic, the concentrated, carefully wrought, gemlike lyric, whose mastery of ambiguity, of allusion, of compressed syntax, of the lyric outburst, is a central concern.

There is one last association which may be made for Miss Dickinson, though it is more difficult of isolation: that is in her marvellous use of nature imagery. Whether one sees this as the product of the influence of Americans, Bryant and Thoreau among others, or of the English Romantics, does not matter significantly. The point is that Miss Dickinson does seem particularly sensitive to the natural world about her. She portrays herself as nature's child, communicating in verse what nature had taught her (note the discussion of the nature theme later in this same section).

As to the character of her verse, it is highly compressed, compact, shy, as if the poet fears above all being seen too fully or dreads the swift rushing on of time which will not allow her to say all that she might wish (though she wrote in lyric #543: "I fear a man of frugal speech"). But more than that, her style is elliptical, often asking of her reader that he fill out the syntax. She will say no more than she must, and at times two or three words will stand for ten or fifteen. While supporting our impression of the poet as parsimonious of speech, hesitant to speak her mind fully, ellipsis also creates often the disturbed state of mind or the child's world, where the rigid requirements of grammatical fullness are ignored. At times too, ambiguously, it suggests either a quality of uncertainty or one of finality.

Her lyrics are highly subjective, rigorously personal. Clark Griffith notes that one-fifth of them begin with *I* (and perhaps an even larger portion of her best lyrics start that way). She knows no other consciousness, except on that rare occasion when she enters the role of a New England lad or assumes the shroud of the neighboring dead. We have been taught always that the lyric is subjective, personal, vibrant with emotion. Emily Dickinson's lyrics support that assumption throughout. (Note: Emily Dickinson often uses *myself* where we would anticipate *I*; she may intend an air of shyness or reluctance in the usage.)

Another frequent characteristic of Miss Dickinson's lyrics is the ambiguity both of meaning and syntax (though it is impossible to imagine either semantic or syntactic ambiguity arising without the one affecting the other). Note, for instance, lyric #98, "One dignity delays for all," where the conflict within the poet's own mind is projected in the ambiguous "How pomp. . . ." Often the bewilderment of mind is forcefully unveiled in the moment of seeming syntactic or semantic indecision. Such ambiguities caused Higginson to write: "She almost always grasped whatever she sought, but with some fracture of grammar and dictionary on the way."

A further characteristic of the lyrics is their concreteness. It is nearly a theorem of lyric poetry that it is as good as it is concrete. Even when she is talking of the most abstract of subjects, Emily Dickinson usually specifies it by elaborating it in the concreteness of simile or metaphor (as in #341, "After great pain, a formal feeling comes"), or she dramatizes it forcibly, letting her actors parade through a dramatic scene to give us a sensory representation of it (as in lyric #712, "Because I could not stop for death," where the afternoon ride in Immortality's carriage is meant to suggest the cycle of life, death, and eternity). Every sense is asked to participate in the imaginative evocation.

Among the poetic forms and devices which the poet uses, the common, long, and short measures of Dr. Watts' hymnals are the chief metric patterns used by Emily Dickinson; alliteration, assonance, and consonance are the chief phonetic means. She exploits particularly the harsh cacophony of the sibilant sounds, sometimes piling them densely into the phonetic pattern to suggest grief or shock or fear or loneliness, sometimes to create onomatopoetic effects (as in #465, "I heard a fly buzz when I died"). She understands that the lyric is to be recited, to be sung, to be heard and marvelled at by the ear as well as by the eye. The total phonetic structure of the lyrics is often worked out in detail, one or two consonants dominating the whole (much as the c [k] and d sounds do in #997, "Crumbling is not an instant's act"). Fundamental too to her poetic art is the use of dissonant rime, rimes which startle us unconsciously by their failure to satisfy expectations which they excite (almost any of the lyrics will serve to illustrate this).

Obscurity is the charge frequently levelled at Miss Dickinson's verse. Higginson had said very early: ". . . she was obscure, and sometimes inscrutable; and though obscurity is sometimes, in Coleridge's phrase, a compliment to the reader, yet it is never safe to press this compliment too hard." It is true that a number of the lyrics defy the best attempts at explication (as do #754, "My life had stood a loaded gun," and #1068, "Further in summer than the birds"), but that is not generally so. At times it is only the rough state of the text (and particularly its want of logical punctuation) which hinders the reader. Once these alienating oddities have been gotten over, the lyric renders its meaning fairly quickly to the careful reader. Of course, what is sometimes labelled obscurity is only the result of an inevitable juggling with word order, a process fundamental to the metric discipline. At times too obscurity is the archway to other meanings or significance which go beyond the more obvious sense of a passage. And, I frankly admit, at times the obscurity is the product of the poet's own willfulness, the covert and idiosyncratic expression of the psychic tangle which results from her wrestling with the trials of her own experience and transforming them through the creative process into art.

Significantly, a few themes occupied the poet: love, nature, doubt and faith, suffering, death, immortality. What Donne had called the great granite obsessions of humankind. While an account of her lonely, isolated existence makes one think of the spinster, Emily Dickinson appears to have loved deeply, perhaps as only those who have "loved and lost" can love, with the intensity of desire which can never be fulfilled in the reality of the lovers' touch. In lyric #511 ("If you were coming in the fall"), she describes the anguish of not knowing when or whether ever she can see her lover again. Yet she can speak as well of love's fulfillment, as in lyric #568 (We learned the whole of love") or #549 ("That I did always love"). Or she could see love in the larger cosmic pattern as the antithesis of hate, the little creative toil of her life which would make living worthwhile (note lyric #478, "I had no time to hate"). (Other examples include numbers 47, 293, 299, 303, 453, 463, 494, 640, 664, 907.)

A fascination with nature consumed Emily Dickinson as well. She summed all her lyrics as "the simple news that nature told," and asked her fellow mortals to judge her tenderly, knowing her love of the natural landscape. In an early lyric (#140, "An altered look about the hills"), she catalogued the wondrous beauties of spring, the landscape alive again with radiant light, newly born as Nicodemus was to have been in Christ's allegory of redemption. She loved "nature's creatures," no matter how insignificant they may have appeared —the robin, the hummingbird, the bee, the butterfly, the rat. In a very late lyric (#1356—"The rat is the concisest tenant"), for example, she celebrated the rodent's ingenuity in taking his living at our expense, but eluding our designs on him. Only the serpent, of all of nature's family, gave her a chill, a feeling which she dramatizes in the role of a lad coming suddenly upon the snake (#986—"A narrow fellow in the grass"). She does at times too reveal a moment of unanticipated terror, as in the strangely symbolic encapsulation of psychic and emotional fear, lyric #520, "I started early, took my dog" (it was composed likely in her year of crisis, 1862). (Other examples include numbers 12, 130, 214, 285, 318, 321, 322, 328, 333, 441, 526, 630, 783, 861, 1084, 1463, 1575.)

In speaking of Miss Dickinson's lyrics on the themes of doubt and faith, let me start by saying her theological orientation was Puritan. She was taught, as a child, all the premises of Calvinistic dogma. She reacted strenuously particularly against two of them: infant damnation and God's sovereign election of His own. There was another force alive in her time that competed for her interests: that was the force of literary transcendentalism which, while it stressed the spiritual values over the material values, still relied too heavily upon intuition and the inner light and denied the authority of revelation. Consequently, we find in Miss Dickinson a kind of paradoxical or at least ambivalent attitude toward matters religious. She disliked Jonathan Edwards, though her letters are filled with enthusiasm for many among the local ministers and their sermons. She loved to speak of a compassionate Savior and of the grandeur of the Scriptures, but she disliked the hypocrisy and arbitrariness which she thought she saw in the institutional church. She praised the Biblical teaching of love, but resisted the *thou shalt nots,* saying that all men could be drawn to Christ if they could see Him as infinitely merciful. She faced honestly the problem of a mortal creature and immortal God, and she was frustrated that she could not understand Him fully in her mortality; yet she continually sought to know Him.

She tells us in one of her lyrics that she approached God in prayer, but as she began to contemplate His magnificence, His infinitude, His creative powers, she could only worship, she could not pray (#564 —"My period had come for prayer"). She was struck over and over again with the incomprehensibility of His power, a power which left her only too aware also of her own finiteness and her own want of power and capacity. At times she came to God in great confidence of spirit and faith, as in lyric #1052, "I never saw a moor." But some have found this utterance of faith contradicted by a companion sense of intimacy with God, an intimacy which often breaks down all barriers or sense of distance for her. She begins one of her most extraordinary prayers: "Papa above" (#61), a salutation which strikes us as hardly appropriate for entrance into the presence of infinity. In another of her tenderest prayers, she addresses Him pogressively as "Burglar, Banker, Father" (#49). There is, however, nothing really irreverent here, but instead a sense of dependence upon God and a desire to feel an intimacy with Him like that which she feels toward others who are very close to her.

There are other lyrics which express grave doubt: #338 ("I know that He exists"), for example, begins in confidence, but ends in despair. Her certainty is swept away by the faint possibility that she has merely deceived herself in her spiritual confidence. This is another of the lyrics of 1862, that year of emotional turmoil and psychic depression, when her world collapsed. In still another quatrain, she looks upon faith as a mere invention (#185, "Faith is a fine invention"). And in still another, she quarrels with God obliquely, disappointed in His not having answered her prayers (#376—"Of course I prayed"). (Other examples include numbers 59, 217, 254, 324, 357, 437, 1207, 1545.)

To speak of Emily Dickinson's obsession with the theme of suffering, let me say that she was singularly sensitive to pain. The sufferings of her friends and of her family half-frightened, half-intrigued her. She seems not to have had unendurable physical sufferings of her own (except perhaps late in life), but she did frequently experience long periods of psychic depression at the losses of friends, family, and neighbors in death. Yet lyric #561, "I measure every grief I meet," shows the analytic fascination which human suffering held for her. What strikes us as odd in the lyric is the eagerness with which she examines the grief of others, probing at their natures and comparing their anguish to hers. Poets have suffered for centuries, and they have written of their sufferings in infinitely varied ways, but how odd for Emily Dickinson to probe so analytically into the nature of grief. Like Robert Burton who, in his *Anatomy of Melancholy,* probed the darker recesses of melancholy, the poet, in her own succinct way, wishes to look at grief, to measure it, to calculate it, to intellectualize it as fully as possible. Her last stanzas become, in fact, a catalog of grief and its causes: death, want, cold, despair, exile. These are the fashions of the cross which the poet explores to find if others suffer as she does, and in that common human bond of grief, to find comfort.

Miss Dickinson could describe the moment of anguish perfectly. She does so in lyric #341, "After great pain, a formal feeling comes." Again, in lyric #241, "I like a look of agony," she builds her meaning upon a poetic lie: her love of the sights of agony and death. Yet that lyric contains an undeniable "truth": for all the grotesqueness we observe in suffering, it does bespeak the genuine. (Other examples include numbers 165, 193, 252, 258, 280, 305, 315, 348, 365, 410, 412, 510, 512, 536, 650, 675, 772, 1005).

And Emily Dickinson wrote perceptively on the theme of death. For thousands of readers, in fact, it has been Miss Dickinson's extraordinary ability to probe the fact of human death that has intrigued them. Her confrontation of the large question of mortality has arrested the minds of a multitude of literary critics and common readers alike. Oddly enough, she often adopts the pose of having already died before she writes her lyric (as she does in #712, "Because I could not stop for death," and #465, "I heard a fly buzz when I died"). If we may engage, for the moment, in what Coleridge called "the willing suspension of disbelief," we shall conclude that writing from such a point of vantage would give the poet much greater authority and lend her testimony stronger credibility. That is true in both of these lyrics, if our artistic imaginations will allow us to indulge the basic dishonesty of the stance.

The grim vision of death too sometimes possesses Emily Dickinson. She can look straight at it and convey the quiet terror of the moment, as she does in lyric #1100, "The last night that she lived." The same starkness haunts lyric #547, "I've seen a dying eye." At other times she can look upon death at a slight distance, describing its external signs with seeming candor (as in #389, "There's been a death in the opposite house"). (Other examples include numbers 49, 88, 98, 153, 182, 301, 360, 369, 411, 529, 784, 856, 976, 1078, 1624, 1716, 1732.)

Emily Dickinson does not leave the dead in their graves. We saw in lyric #712 that the horses' heads faced eternity. Now, in lyric #216, "Safe in their alabaster chambers," she describes the meek members of the resurrection. Nonetheless, we must not think again that she held always so optimistically to the promise of life everlasting. She could express doubt in her speculations upon immortality too. Another lyric of that crisis year, 1862, contains the antithesis to the consolation of philosophy (#301, "I reason, earth is short"). Yet perhaps one of the most compelling of her lyrics on immortality is that in which she expresses enduring confidence and hope, #615, "Our journey had advanced." Her final conviction on the subject is elusively paradoxical. (Other examples include numbers 401, 409, 413, 829, 964.)

Thus the poet, shy, eccentric, withdrawn from the conventional realities we treasure so dearly, exulting in the visions of the mind, giving her attentions to love and nature, doubt and faith, suffering, death, and immortality, those timely obsessions of the human heart, achieved a richness of life, a depth of imaginative speculation which few mortals achieve.

Poem-by-Poem Analysis

(A first-line index of these poems will be found at the end of this volume.)

The Morns Are Meeker Than They Were (12)*

The approach of autumn is the theme of this brief lyric, alive with bright personifications of morning, berry, rose, maple, and field. The splendid dawns of summer, rendering the hillsides of New England alive with excitement, are ended. The quiet natural beauty of later summer and early fall take the landscape, stirring the poet's very being, inspiring her own participation in its gaity. She will discard the "old" fashions of the earlier season and share in nature's quiet exuberance, wearing some small "trinket" as the sign of her response to it (note that, in the nineteenth century, *trinket* did not necessarily have the trivial sense it does today, but referred simply to an ornament of jewelry).

The poem (entitled "Autumn" when it first appeared in *Poems,* 1890) illustrates a familiar pattern in nature poetry: the poet serving at first as observer, registering the sights and sounds of the landscape, recording its atmosphere, but finally drawn into the natural setting, becoming a part of the scene she is describing.

Skillfully Miss Dickinson structures her delightful musical evocation: the alliteration of *m* sounds in line 1 subdues the tone in a way which matches the meekness of the new autumn mornings; the repetition of *scar-* from *scarf* (line 5) to *scarlet* (line 5) underscores the adjective, impressing upon our minds the fiery radiance of the field. The latter effect is increased by the surrounding repetition of *g* and

---

* All numbers are those assigned the lyrics by Thomas H. Johnson in his three-volume *Poems of Emily Dickinson,* Cambridge, Massachusetts: The Belknap Press of Harvard University Press, 1955, and are used by permission.

f sounds in lines 5-7. The triple *t* sound of the last line captures the adolescent gaity of the speaker, seeking with some trifle to match the landscape's beauty. The use of a single rime (*brown-town-gown-on*) binds the lyric tightly together, but avoids too obvious a simplicity by the slight dissonance of the imperfect concluding rime (*on*).

The meter of the two stanzas has a remarkably simple lilt, capturing the rapture of the child experiencing the progress of the seasons with a new awareness and enthusiasm. It is only the loss of an accented syllable at the ends of lines 3 and 7 that keeps the lyric from a monotonous sing-song:

        lines 1 and 5:   x/   x/   x/   x/
        lines 2 and 6:   x/   x/   x/
        lines 3 and 7:   x/   x/   x/   x(/)
        lines 4 and 8:   x/   x/   x/

In both stanzas, the first line is the longest, bringing us to attention, then allowing us a swifter motion through the succeeding verses. The *maple* (line 5) of the second stanza catches the alliteration of the opening line again, serving as a recapitulation.

Having made persons of natural objects and events, the poet concludes by merging her person with the landscape.

Heart! We Will Forget Him! (47)

The lyric is a monolog addressed by the mind to the heart, working out its strategy for forgetting a lover. The mind, full of the memories of the radiant light of his intellect, asks the advice and aid of heart, still feeling his emotional heat, both engaged in the ironic struggle to forget him. Mind starts its utterance with full assurance, determined to forget him and that immediately; but before the lyric is done, mind is frustrated by the intrusion of his memory.

We may only speculate upon the person of the poet's lover. He may have been Ben Newton, Miss Dickinson's father's law apprentice, who had moved to Worcester, Massachusetts, in 1850, married, and died of consumption a few months later. Emily Dickinson had designated him her "friend who taught me Immortality." She had treasured his friendship as a rare breath of intellectual stimulation in her drab New England circumstance.

Or she may be alluding to the Rev. Charles Wadsworth, the renowned Philadelphia clergyman whom she had met on her return from Washington in 1855. She had perhaps taken his solicitation too seriously, mistaking his spiritual counsel and concern for love. In the depth of her troubled soul she strove to put her love of him out of her mind.

The meter of the lyric is highly irregular, marked by sudden stops and starts, conveying the anguish which she feels in struggling to banish his memory:

```
    (x)/   /x  x/   x(/)
    (x)/   x/  x/
    /x  x/  x/  x/
    /x  x/  x/
5   x/  x/  //  x(/)
    x/  x/  x/
    (x)/  x/  x/  x(/)
    (x)/  x/  x/
```

The number of prosodic elisions is large for so brief a lyric, and the number of trochaic feet (/x) is unusual as well for Miss Dickinson's poetry. Yet the effect is not gratuitous. It reinforces the psychological confusion and struggle remarkably.

The effects of sound echoings are equally stirring. Note, for example, how *haste* (line 7) takes us back to the emphasis of *heart* (line 1). Note too the parallel syntactic and semantic structures of lines 3 and 4 (except for the last two words of 3) and the emphasis brought by the placing of *you* (line 5) and *I* (line 6) in identical second-syllable slots in the lines.

Here too, as in numerous of the lyrics, a slight blemish in the rime (*begin-him* in lines 6 and 8) conveys a quality of bewilderment suitable to the intent of the lines, the *lagging* adding to the confusion by its phonological kinship to *begin*.

I Never Lost as Much But Twice (49)

The poet, bereft a third time of one she loves, casts herself once more upon the bosom of God. At first she accuses Him boldly—He has stolen an object she prizes dearly. He has burglarized her. But suddenly she recognizes Him as her benefactor, the banker who reimburses her store, making up in some way to her for His theft. And at last she addresses Him in the tenderest of all epithets, as her Father, ready to receive her in the crisis of spiritual poverty.

An interesting ambiguity has been noted, one which turns on the word *that* and upon the ellipsis surrounding it. Does the poet mean to say that these two losses were in the sod (that is, the grave), while this is not in death? Or that those other two losses were also in the sod? Of course, our determination of the solution of the ambiguity will affect the biographical interpretation of the poem. The former reading would suggest perhaps that this third loss is the going of Wadsworth to California, a loss as great to her as the deaths of, say, Sophia Holland and Ben Newton.

The cacophonous effect of the words is carried partly by the triple repetition of the word *twice,* its *s* sound reinforced by that of such other words as *lost* (line 1), *sod* (line 2,) *stood* (line 3), *descending* (line 5), *reimbursed, store* (line 6), and *once* (line 8). The meter moves with a steady regularity, interrupted by elided syllables at the ends of lines 3, 5, and 7, and at the beginnings of lines 5, 6, and 7. The last line strengthens the force of the meaning by clustering three accented syllables together, emphasizing poverty's return:

```
    x/   x/   x/   x/
    x/   x/   x/
    /x   x/   x/   x(/)
    x/   x/   x/
5  (x)/  x/   x/   x(/)
   (x)/  x/   x/
   (x)/  x/   x/   x(/)
    xx   //   /(?)
```

The lyric derives part of its poignant simplicity from the straightforward dramatization, the helpless victim forced to approach the door of Him who has wronged her so sorely, compelled to cast herself upon His mercy, and the tender Father, receiving His broken child and comforting her with angelic consolation after she has blamed Him.

A Little East of Jordan (59)

This compact lyric is based on the Biblical account of the patriarch Jacob's wrestling with the angel of God (or perhaps with an incarnation of God in human or angelic form). The incident is recorded in Genesis XXXII: 24-32. Jacob, fleeing his angry brother Esau (whom he had earlier swindled out of his birthright), wrestled all night with an angel, refusing to release the heavenly messenger until the angel had blessed him. The angel did bless Jacob, changing his name from Jacob ("supplanter") to Israel ("a prince with God"). Jacob named the spot Penial ("seeing God"), since he had confronted God face to face.

Miss Dickinson's account is, as I suggested earlier, compact and elliptical, requiring some agility in her reader. Her "Till morning touching mountain," for example, is her description of dawn, and the angel's desire "to breakfast" may suggest his double desire both to revitalize himself by eating at dawn and to "break" the "fast" hold Jacob has upon him. There is some doubt too as to the exact implication of "stranger"; is it the title Jacob gives to the angel as he speaks to him, or is the meaning: (and what may seem even) stranger, (the Angel) acceded to (Jacob's request)?

The poem concludes somewhat ironically—while the patriarch seems to have triumphed over God, he is nonetheless bewildered by the entire experience. That bewilderment is conveyed in the dissonance of the rimes, each stanza slightly disappointing our expectation (*record-hard, strong-return, go-to, beyond-God*).

Papa Above! (61)

As reverent as Emily Dickinson could be at times in approaching God, she could come to Him too with a degree of flippancy. Obsessed by the humiliation of her position, she adopts the allegorical mask of a frightened mouse, harassed by a fiendish cat (the tribulations of the day? some disagreeable human association?). She longs to be allowed some heavenly cupboard in which to hide herself and in which to find the scraps of cheese and crumbs by which to sustain herself.

The chief figurative effect of the lyric is its underplay of the grand conceptions of its theme—a troubled human being casting herself upon God in hope of attaining immortality. The solemnity of the religious motif is destroyed altogether in the "puckish" allegory. The tone is not necessarily irreverent, but it is playful, converting serious theological concepts into a child's world of imagination: the heavenly Father becomes "Papa above," the mansions of the eternal city become a mortal dwelling infested with mice (or at least with one mouse-rat), the all-sufficient graciousness of God becomes the cup-

board which the mouse has invaded and where he will dwell throughout the cycle of eternity.

While the lyric has been set down in nine lines, it is actually only
eight, the first two forming a normal tetrameter line:

```
    /x   x/
              x/   x/
    x/   x/   x/
    x/   x/   x/   x(/)
 5  x/   x/   x/

    /x   x/   x/   x(/)
    x/   x/   x/
    x/   x/   x/   x(/)
    //   x/   x/
```

Success Is Counted Sweetest (67)

No one comprehends the sweetness of victory so well as the man
who has experienced the anguish of defeat. This statement, supported
by a brief and an extended illustration, is the subject of the lyric. To
appreciate fully the deliciousness of a sweet beverage requires that
one be indeed thirsty.

The expanded illustration of the lyric's theme is a dramatization of
defeat. The purple host of victorious soldiers do not comprehend the
wonder of their triumph so well as does the soldier lying defeated,
near death, on the field of battle. He hears the distant shouts of victory and feels the reality of it much more sharply.

There is here, as in numerous other of Miss Dickinson's lyrics, an
example of syntactic ambiguity. The word *clear* (line 8) is inflected
as an adjective (the adverbial form would be *clearly*), while it functions in an adverbial slot. The combining of the two parts of speech
into a single form and its placement achieves a double effect, suggesting both that the victor cannot give so clear a definition of victory
(the adjectival sense) and that he cannot tell the definition so clearly
(the adverbial sense). In the first case it is the noun which is defined,
in the second the verb. Miss Dickinson achieves both by a kind of
lyric compression.

The lyric weaves its sounds skillfully in the creation of a mood
appropriate to the concluding scene of defeat. The hissing of the

opening lines creates a definite cacophonous quality (*success-sweetest-succeed-sorest*) which is echoed in the concluding lines (*distant-strains-burst*). The repetition of the *d* sound in key words in stanzas two and three serves as well to draw special attention to them, causing us to weigh their meanings carefully (*definition-defeated-dying-forbidden-distant-agonized*).

While the lyric is brief, it is never allowed to move very swiftly, the clusters of consonant sounds requiring care in the oral recitation (*counted sweetest by*, lines 1-2; *requires sorest need*, line 4; *the distant strains of triumph burst*, lines 11-12). The omissions of accented syllables at the ends of lines 1, 3, 7, 9, and 11 require as well their due in silence:

```
        x/   x/   x/   x(/)
        x/   x/   x/
        x/   x/   x/   x(/)
        x/   x/   x/
  5     //   x/   x/   x/
        x/   x/   x/
        x/   x/   x/   x(/)
        x/   x/   x/
        x/   x/   x/   x(/)
 10     x/   x/   x/
        x/   x/   x/   x(/)
        //   x/   x/
```

Exultation Is the Going (76)

As a poet, Emily Dickinson was vitally interested in words. Often her lyrics are efforts at definition. But her method is never that of the lexicographer; it is always that of the poet, striving to give concrete shape to an abstract term. Here it is *exultation* which she seeks thus to define (in *Poems,* 1890, it was given the title "Setting Sun"). A dictionary of her own era may have said of the word: "lively joy, great gladness, rapturous delight." But the poet must dramatize. To her exultation is the first voyage of a mainlander into the vast eternity of the sea.

Having spent nearly all her years inland, remote from any large body of water, Emily Dickinson selects the image of voyage as illustrative of the powerful delight of exultation. Her second stanza is built upon the contrast between her own feelings of rapture at the first moments offshore and those of the sailor, who, accustomed as he is to the water, must take the experience for granted. One can know the intoxicating joy of exultation only by experiencing it for oneself.

The poet creates a sense of the intoxication in the very lapse of syntax. *Bred as we* strictly modifies *the sailor,* but the clear contrast between the poet and the sailor suggests: "Can the sailor understand this experience as fully as do we who were bred among the mountains inland?" The solecism thus underscores the agitated state of mind within the speaker.

The metric scheme of the lyric is unusually irregular as Dickinson scansion goes:

```
    xx/   x/   x/   x(/)
    xx/   x/   x/
    /x   /x   /x   /x
    xx/   x/   x/
5   /x   /x   /x   /x
    xx/   x/   x/
    xx/   x/   x/   x(/)
    xx/   //   x/
```

Lines 1, 2, 4, 6, 7, and 8 start with anapestic feet, creating an effect of surge at the beginnings of each of them. There is a rush into the line, a burst of prosodic energy which undergirds the description of the experience. Line 3 is composed of four trochaic feet which progress steadily in observation of sights passing at the voyage's start, houses and the projections of land into the sea. The last line contains a startling effect in the three clustered accents "first league out," but the emphasis derived from the grouping supports the meaning.

The use of three words, *soul* (line 2), *eternity* (line 4), and *divine* (line 7), lead some to allegorize the voyage metaphor. Perhaps Emily Dickinson wishes us to think really of some spiritual exultation, the finite soul in contemplation of eternity, of God, of the Infinite. It is, of course, possible that she selected the words only for their hyperbolic effect; their broader implications are nonetheless suggestive.

As by the Dead We Love To Sit (88)

The lyric is one of Emily Dickinson's best, though omitted from Johnson's *Final Harvest.* Its elliptical syntax creates considerable difficulty for the reader. The difficulty is in no sense gratuitous, however. Here, as in numerous other of her lyrics, she uses the distraught, convoluted syntax, as well as the semantic ambiguities, to recreate in her readers the disturbed, bewildered state of mind of which the lyric is an embodiment.

The whole fabric of the poem is a series of poetic lies which, in sum, total a kind of artistic truth. We do not love to sit at the bedside of a dying friend; yet we do love to in the sense that we would find it intolerable not to have been near to comfort when he died. And our dilemma is apparent in the illogic of our behavior: we care more for one lost than for all we possess, though only in loss does the "wondrous dear"-ness become apparent.

What is the matter with us? Has our system of calculation broken down? Surely the possession of "all the rest" more than compensates us for this one loss. But again the estimate is itself a lie: no system of cold computation can give consolation at this dark moment. Our whole mathematic has broken under the strain of grief.

Miss Dickinson ostensibly diverts our attention from the conventions of grief, the tears and sentimentality, by the language of statistics. Yet the very device itself becomes the means of her oblique intensification of the sorrow, while allowing her an evasion of morbidity. Even the metaphor does not do what it seems to do, but deceives us into allowing it to make its point indirectly.

The last line brings us back abruptly to the proper hypocritical exaggeration, the necessary euphemism which enables us to endure ourselves and to bear the anguish of loss in death. We are not *stingy* (the straightforward term); our eyes are *penurious:* destitute, impoverished, and so, rightly greedy of loss.

The syntax as well contributes to the obliquity of the lines. Two dangling adverbial clauses compose the first stanza, while ellipsis of connectives makes precise syntactic interpretation impossible in the second. The syntactic incompleteness is no hindrance, however; instead, it conveys with immediacy the state of mind of the bereaved. At each step we fear we have made a false move, but each move finds confirmation of its rightness as the poem progresses.

One Dignity Delays for All (98)

Here Emily Dickinson brilliantly describes the external circumstances of a nineteenth-century funeral: the coach, the footman, the chamber in which the corpse lies in state, the throng of mourners, the somber bells which resound as the body is borne along toward the grave, the stiff ceremoniousness of those who stand alongside the casket, the grandeur and solemnity of the funeral service itself; each part of the proceeding is evoked in steady, rapid sequence. All is shrouded about with a proper reverence of tone, and there is an almost rhapsodic note in the voice when we arrive at the concluding stanza to see ourselves in regal ermine, raised to such nobility in death.

However, upon reconsideration of the details of the lyric, there is one syntactic ambiguity which arises, affecting the tone of the entire poem. That is in line 13: "How pomp surpassing ermine." *Pomp* is, in inflection (grammatical form), a noun. However, it is placed in a syntactic slot where one would anticipate an adjective: "How pompous." The difficulty arises in the connotative contrasts between the nounal and adjectival forms. The noun *pomp* may suggest a stately and dignified display of magnificence; however, the adjective *pompous* suggests usually an exaggeration, a pretentiousness, a rancid show of pageantry. Thus, if the noun is held to, the lyric is a simple picture of the grandness of a funereal exercise, but if the adjective is insisted upon, the lyric becomes an ironic comment on the excesses of funereal practice.

The elliptical syntax of the concluding stanza compels us to fill out the logic of the passage in one of two ways:

Noun: "How (great a) pomp (there will be, even) surpassing (the) ermine (of kings)."

Adjective: "How pomp(ous an event that will be,) surpassing (the pompousness of kings in their) ermine."

Upon that choice will rest our reading of the entire poem, either as a sincere and appreciative picture of the dignified pomp of the funeral or as a parody of the hypocrisy and mocking excesses of the funereal gaudiness which accompanies the ending of human life.

The question will arise in some minds whether two such disparate meanings can comfortably coexist within the same passage or whether the resultant ambivalence is only a confusion in need of clarification. It appears, nonetheless, that Miss Dickinson has captured the ambiguities of feeling we all experience when we think of the ceremonies of death. All who stand at the graveside know how essential is the dignity of the moment; yet, paradoxically, we are often struck as well by the embarrassing hypocrisy of the rite. Emily Dickinson compresses that contradiction into the very syntax of her lyric.

The meter of the lyric is unusual, containing a large number of spondaic feet, which give the poem its gravity and slow pace:

```
        //  xx  x/  x/
        //  x/  x/
        /x  x/  //  x(/)
        (x)/  x/  //
   5    /x  x/  x/  x(/)
        /x  x/  x/
        //  xx  x/  x(/)
        x/  //  x/
        //  xx  x/  x(/)
  10    //  x/  x/
        //  xx  x/  x(/)
        //  x/  x/
        //  x/  x/  x(/)
        x/  x/  x/
  15    x/  //  x/  x(/)
        x/  x/  x/
```

There is throughout a remarkable array of emphatic monosyllables, from the first resounding rimes at the starts of each line in the first stanza (*one-one-none-none*), an effect heard faintly again in the *what-what-how-how* of lines 9, 10, 11, 13, to the staunch dignity of *crown* (line 4), *coach* (line 5), *state, throng* (line 6), *bells* (line 7), *pomp* (line 13), and *rank* (line 16), each requiring effort in enumeration because of the starting and stopping consonant sounds.

In addition, there are arresting echoes of sound as in *dignity-delays* (line 1), *avoid-evade* (lines 3-4), *crown-coach* (lines 4-5), *hundred-hats* (line 12), *surpassing-simple* (lines 13-14), *pause-parting-surpassing-simple-present* (lines 10, 11, 13, 14, 15), *meek-escutcheon-claim-rank* (lines 15-16).

To Fight Aloud Is Very Brave (126)

Of the two varieties of conflict, the spectacular battle of arms and the silent struggle within the spirit of man, the latter is, to Emily Dickinson's mind, the gallanter. While she does not belittle the fierce show of arms in the field (it requires that one be "very brave"), the strife of soul demands far greater courage. Again the poet dramatizes the soul's contest, using the battlefield as its metaphor: the cavalry's charge, the victory, the defeat—yet none observe or honor those patriots who engage in such a conflict, unless perhaps it be the angels who see and applaud such heroism, parading joyously in heaven for such.

The highly compressed form which the lyric takes creates a number of unusual but effective passages. The opening line, for example, is odd not only in its predication, but in its use of the word *aloud* as well. An expanded version might read: "To fight aloud (that is, with the noise and display of actual war) is (an action which requires that a man be) very brave, but (they are even) gallanter who charge, etc." The inversion of the third stanza also often misleads the reader newly come to the lyric: "We trust (that) the angels go (that is, parade) in plumed procession for (or, in honor of) such (persons as those who fight their spiritual battle, parading) rank after rank with even feet (that is, in a perfectly rehearsed march) and (bedecked with) uniforms of snow." My expanded "translation" is, as poetry goes, vastly inferior to the original compact version, but it does reveal the process of mind necessary to fill out the semantic implications of the passage.

The lyric is highly regular in meter, following the frequent pattern of alternating iambic tetrameters and iambic trimeters (common measure). There are the irregularities of omitted accented syllables at the ends of lines 3, 7, and 9 (creating the effect of brief necessary pauses in the scansion), and the trochaic substitution at the start of line 11 (giving emphasis to the word *rank* and starting the procession with a strong left foot).

The rimes of the first and last stanzas are perfect, while that of the second stanza is dissonant, perhaps suggesting the sadness of the dying eyes of the soul destroyed by the conflict without so much as a regard from his fellows. It seems particularly ironical that the dissonance should hover about the word *love,* since the want of human compassion is indeed what makes the trial of soul more difficult.

There are distinct subtleties of sound organization in the lyric, the assonance of *dying eyes* (line 7) and *even feet* (line 11), along with the assonantal riming of *trust* (line 9) and *such* (line 10), placed in the first accented-syllable positions of the two lines. A similar harmony is achieved in the use of the alliterative *nations* (line 5) and *none* (line 6) in the second accented-syllable positions of those lines, an effect greatly enhanced by the use of identical syntactic (subject-verb) structures in contrasting semantic (win-fall) passages: *who win* (line 5)—*who fall* (line 6).

These Are the Days When Birds Come Back (130)

Called by its first editors "Indian Summer" (*Poems,* 1890), this lyric records the events of a warm, bright summer spell in the midst of autumn. The beauty of Indian summer almost persuades the natural and human creatures that it is June again, leading the poet to offer a prayer in which she asks to be made a part of an eternal summer.

The vision itself is momentary, the brief confusion of the birds who return to see if they were perhaps mistaken at the coming cold, the seeming deception of the skies, taking again their summer appearance. The bee cannot be deceived, though the poet very nearly can—until the seeds blown about by the wind and the first falling leaf remind her that summer has ended.

At that instant, Indian summer becomes a religious rite, the last Eucharistic moment in which the child-poet may share the bliss of summer. At the conclusion, the scene takes on an allegorical cast in which the summer represents youth, and the autumn all that threatens it. The aging poet (Miss Dickinson is now twenty-nine) sees the vitality of youth stealing away and beseeches it to stay.

This lyric is unusual in that it is arranged in three-line stanzas with an unusual rime scheme:

	scansion					rime word	scheme
	/x	x/	x/	x/		(back)	a
	x/	x/	x/	x/	(few)	(two)	b-b
	x/	x/	x/			(look)	a
	/x	x/	x/	x/		(-sume)	c
5	x/	//	x/	x/		(June)	c
	x/	x/	x/			(-take)	a
	x/	x/	x/	x/		(bee)	d
	x/	x/	x/	x/		(-ty)	d
	x/	x/	x/			(-lief)	e
10	x/	x/	x/	x/		(bear)	f
	x/	x/	x/	x/		(air)	f
	/x	x/	x/			(leaf)	e
	x/	x/	x/	x/		(days)	g
	x/	x/	x/	x/		(haze)	g
15	x/	x/	x/			(join)	h

x/ x/ x/ x/	(-take)	i (a₁)
x/ x/ x/ x/	(take)	i (a₁)
x/ x/ x/	(wine)	h

Each stanza has two iambic tetrameter lines followed by a third iambic trimeter, the six stanzas paired off by the rime into three sets of two stanzas each. The rimes are all imperfect, except b, d, f, and g, with two examples of repetition (e and i). Rimes a and h contain consonant echoes (*k* and *n*), while rime c contains a vowel echo (*u*).

There are other effects of sound, the alliteration of *b*irds-*b*ack (line 1), *b*ird (line 2), *b*ackward (line 3), *b*lue (line 6), *b*ee (line 7), and *b*elief (line 9); the rime of *old-old* (line 5) and *gold* (line 6); the hissing of the sibilants in the last three stanzas (rank*s*-*s*eed*s*-witne*ss*-*s*oftly-hurrie*s*-*s*acrament-*s*ummer-day*s*-la*s*t-haze-*s*acred-emblem*s*-con*s*ecrated), an effect which forces upon us the harsh reality of summer's end.

An Altered Look About the Hills (140)

When it first appeared in *Poems* (1891), the lyric was entitled by its editors "April." It is, in contrast to lyric #130, a picture of the revival of life on the landscape, the rebirth of nature. The reddish-blue (Tyrian) sky at dawn, the first appearances of fly and spider and flower, the fresh vitality of the rooster's crowing—all the sights and sounds which proclaim the coming of spring—may be seen and heard in Emily Dickinson's New England countryside.

As in the earlier lyric (#130), the revival of the seasons takes on connotations of a religious rite. It was Nicodemus who elicited from Christ the mystery of the new birth: "Marvel not that I said unto you, 'You must be born again!'" (cf. John III:1-21). The spiritual mystery of death and birth, of the winter and spring of the soul, is implicit in those words, a mystery shadowed forth in the seasonal cycle.

Here too is an unusual verse form for Miss Dickinson, the iambic tetrameter couplet, though few of the rimes are perfect (and it is impossible to say how she brought *foot* and *slope* together in lines 5 and 6). Yet its vivid appeal to the senses of sight, sound, and smell have made it a popular lyric.

Dust Is the Only Secret (153)

The subject of death fascinated Emily Dickinson throughout her life. Here she assumes the traditional personification of "him" and anatomizes his behavior. There is about him great mystery, great secrecy. No one can fathom the obscurity which enshrouds him. You cannot find out more about him in his "native land" (the cemetery?), for there no one can speak of him or reveal his identity. "He" seems to appear out of nowhere, has no traceable genealogy, no record of his being or background—the elusive mystery of death.

He is then characterized by certain epithets which describe aspects of his personality, some of which (*sedate,* for example) describe the circumstances of the event and its onlookers as much as they do death. He is so bold as to enter fearlessly any gathering; yet he can work so quietly that he would scarcely be observed. There appears to be only one who can outsmart him—that is Christ. He robs the nest where death would store up its victims, restoring to eternal life and rest those taken by death but trusting in the Son of God.

The metric of the lyric, while it starts out somewhat regularly in an alternating iambic-tetrameter iambic-trimeter pattern, loses its steadiness in stanzas three and four, as if the mystery of death (and its attendant mystery of resurrection) has eluded the very metric form itself:

```
      /x  x/  x/  x(/)
     (x)/ x/  x/
      x/  x/  x/  x/
     (x)/ x/  x/

  5  /x  x/  x/  x(/)
     (x)/ x/  x/
     (x)/ x/  x/  x(/)
      x/  x/  x/

      x/  x/  x/  x(/)
 10 (x)/ xx  x/
      /x  x/  x(/)
     (x)/ x/  x/

     (x)/ xx  //
      //  x/
 15  /x  /x  /x
      /x  x/
```

But as the regularity of meter breaks down, the reliance upon other nuances of sound echoings takes the fore: the bold alliteration of *bold-brigand-builds-bird* and the emphasis gained by the *robs-robin-robin-rest*, reinforced by the *-st* sounds of *Christ* and *nest,* create a harmony of sounds which keep us from noticing too closely the evasive pulsation of the meter.

Just Lost, When I Was Saved! (160)

This lyric was first printed in the Springfield *Independent* (March 12, 1891) and later in *Poems* (1891) with the title "Called Back" assigned to it by its editors. It is the poetic utterance of one who had been at the gate of death and returned to tell what she had seen. Having had barely a glimpse into the mystery of eternity, she was "called back" to tell what she had experienced and to look forward to that final reality of death.

The elliptical quality of the lines conveys the excitement of the speaker of the poem, whose brush with death has given her "secrets" of the unheard, unseen region. To expand the first line, for example, would require: "(I was) just (at the point of being) lost (in death), when I was saved (i. e., brought back to life)!" The world was just about to slip away, the poet set for the journey into eternity, when breath (the tangible symbol of life or spirit) returned, and the tide that has sought to carry her to sea washed offshore without her. Returned from such an experience, she feels like a seaman having discovered a new and strange land or like a newsman overwhelmed by the story he has to tell.

But the experience points forward too, and the poet speaks of her anticipation in breathless ellipsis again: "Next time, (when I approach death and eternity, it will be) to stay! / Next time, (I shall have the opportunity) to see the things / By ear unheard, etc." "Next time, (I shall be asked) to tarry, etc." Her vision of eternity was momentary, but it invited her mind to contemplate her final residence in the regions of death.

The lyric is unusual both in its metric and stanzaic organization and in its rime (abbcdd / eeffe / ghih / jklk):

```
//  x/  x/
//  x/  x/
//  xx  x/  xx  x/  x/
```

```
        x/  //
     5  x/  x/  x/
        x/  x/  x/  x/  x/

        /x  x/  x/  x/
        //  x/  x/  x/
        //  x/  x/  x/
    10  //  x/  xx  x/  x/
        x/  x/

        //  x/
        //  x/  x/
        x/  x/
    15  x/  x/  x/

        //  x/  x(/)
        xx/  x/
        //  x/  x/
        xx/  x/
```

The phonological music of the lyric is complicated and subtle, the *st* sound of *just lost* (line 1) and *just* (lines 2 and 3) being caught in the reversal of *onset* (line 3) and in the *s* of *saved* (line 1) and the *t* of *felt* (line 2) and *girt* (line 3). The slow steady alliteration and stress of the three monosyllables *breath blew back* (line 4) keeps the line from giving up its meaning too quickly, since the action described contains the clue to the return to life. The consonantal echoings of *side* (line 5) in *recede* and *disappointed* (in reverse) and *tide* (line 6) are a part of the skillful arrangement which creates the lyric's aural beauty.

In stanza 2, the repetition of sibilants (*secrets-some-sailor-some*) prepares for the mystic conclusion of the stanza in the *seal* which locks up the secrets of eternity. Her misquotation of I Corinthians II:9 (a verse which does not describe heaven) nonetheless gains its force from the popular misunderstanding of the context and appropriates for the lyric a proper Biblical aura. On and on stretch the ageless centuries of eternity (a concept often illustrated by the endless rim of a wheel).

A Wounded Deer Leaps Highest (165)

Out of suffering or disaster often springs what is most beautiful or awesome in life. No deer of the forest leaps so high as that which has been wounded. It was the rock struck by the patriarch Moses from which the water gushed, etc. Thus in a sequence of concrete illustrations Miss Dickinson implies her thesis. Where the hectic (a troublesome fever characterized by alternating heat, sweat, and chill) "stings," the face is reddest, and where one observes mirth, he should recognize that it is only the protective armor worn by a man experiencing anguish, donned to conceal the bleeding wounds of his grief from the onlooker.

The lyric is a brilliant verbal representation of the various "stricken" states and of their compensating manifestations. Its appeal is primarily to the sense of sight (though there may be a tactual sensation at the point of the fever's sting). Its chief effect is paradox: the deer's leap and the silent brake, the contrast of mirth and anguish. We cannot judge the state of mind or soul by the overt behavior, since the reaction is often ironical to the stimulus.

The metric pattern of the lyric is in keeping with Miss Dickinson's usual pattern: alternating iambic tetrameters and trimeters with frequent loss of final accented syllable of the tetrameter lines (e.g., 1, 5, 7, 9). The one exception is the shortened concluding trimeter line (x // x/), the elided syllable helping to emphasize the spondaic shout "you're hurt."

The orchestration of sounds is again inviting, the alliteration of the *h* sound of the opening stanza (*highest-heard-hunter*) being echoed in the later *h*ectic (line 8) and *h*urt (line 12). The dissonance of the rimes of the first and third stanzas (*tell-still, arm-exclaim*) adding its appropriateness to the harsh sibilants of stanza two (*smitten-gushes-steel-springs-cheek-is-always-just-stings*). The last stanza starts more euphoniously (*mirth-mail*), but gives way quickly too to the cacophony of the preceeding stanza (*anguish-cautious-lest-spy-exclaim*).

If I Shouldn't Be Alive (182)

While only thirty at the time of the writing of the lyric, the poet shows here her ever-present obsession with death. That theme unites with her love of "nature's people," her concern that the robin be given a crumb when he returns in the spring. Emily Dickinson loved her garden and yard, making the birds and the neighborhood children special objects of her care.

The request is made all the more urgent by its being cast as the dying words of the speaker. The speaker's fear of her own death makes her concern for the robin all the more touching. The act is to be a memorial honoring her sleeping corpse. And the benevolent act is to be recognized by the "granite lip" of the dead poet, unable to utter the words, but "trying" to form them in the grave.

There are interesting echoes of sound in the lyric: *If I couldn't* (line 5) answering to *If I shouldn't* (line 1), and the alliteration of *r*obins-*r*ed (lines 2 and 3) and *c*ome-*c*rave*t*-*c*rumb-*c*ouldn't (lines 2-5) binding the short lines neatly together.

Faith Is a Fine Invention (185)

The lyric plays ironically upon the traditional conception that faith is resorted to when we cannot see. It is the skeptic who says "seeing is believing"; the pious man turns to faith when he cannot see or affirm with his senses. There is a cryptic flippancy about the whole, a seeming desire to shock wildly by the unorthodoxy of the point of view. Perhaps we could discover more about the lyric's intention if we knew more of the circumstances which caused Emily Dickinson to include it in a letter to Samuel Bowles.

I Shall Know Why When Time Is Over (193)

At first the poem appears to give a traditional Christian answer to the questions of human anguish: while I do not understand human suffering now, Christ will make it all clear in heaven. However, the poet questions that assertion, suggesting ironically that she won't need to know then; she will have ceased wondering why. The repetition of the last line reinforces our sense of her dissatisfaction with the traditional answer, emphasizing the present reality of her pain—no future forgetting of it can make it any less real *now*.

Even her statement of the "solution" (lines 3-4) is undercut by the cacophony of sibilants (Chri*s*t-explain-each-*s*eparate-anguish-*s*choolroom-*s*ky). And her effort to seek consolation in Peter's promise (the apostle's teaching that the example of Christ's suffering should teach us patient endurance of persecution and pain) is dissipated by the contrast of person *(his-me-me,* lines 6 and 8).

The poem then is built upon the irony of the poet's striving to accept the Christian solution to the problem of pain, all the while contending with the present anguish which would sweep the traditional rationale from her. It is the struggle to find consolation in the midst of unconsolable anguish, to trust despite the mind and body's woe. That irony is conveyed emphatically in the very rimes of the lyric, the perfection of *why-sky* (stanza one) suggesting a momentary consolation, while the dissonance of *woe-now* (stanza two) declares the unsettling evidence of her doubt.

I'm Wife—I've Finished That (199)

When it first appeared in *Poems* (1890), this lyric had been entitled by its editors "Apocalypse." Shaped by Emily Dickinson's delight in pretense and exaggeration, the lyric resolves a double anxiety for the poet. She was frustrated in two desires—one for the love of a husband, the other for assurance of salvation. Here she yokes together the two longings and sees herself as the bride of a mortal lover as well as of Christ. She has found in this "marriage" a consolation and a point of contrast: her former life is a kind of pain as compared to her newfound consolation, her girlhood an "odd" memory contrasted with the assurance of womanly attainment, the heaven achieved, a resounding joy contrasted with the imperfect earth below.

The cryptic statements of the lines are supported by the odd effect of meter and stanza as well as the strange dissonance of all but the final rime (*that-state, now-so, looks-eclipse, so-now, then-pain*). The dimeter lines of stanzas one (lines 2 and 4) and three (lines 11 and 12) give a feeling of abruptness to the passage, a feeling which the poet seems to strive for—she cuts our inquiring minds short by them, refusing to give any more information about her "marriage" than: "I'm Wife! Stop there!"

Come Slowly, Eden! (211)

Entitled by Emily Dickinson's editors "Apotheosis" when it first appeared (*Poems,* 1890), this lyric, along with numerous others, expresses the poet's difficulty in accepting the joyous experience. Pain she can readily tolerate; joy (the experience of Paradise, Eden) tends to unseat her, to set her head spinning. It produces in her something like intoxication.

In describing her experience of delight, Miss Dickinson slips into metaphor and then simile, the elegant, fragrant jasmine flower becoming the concrete embodiment of her joy, she the fainting bee who loses himself in the aromatic nectar of the flower (the figure is palpably erotic in the bee's entrance of the jasmine's chambers and his intoxication with her nectars).

The meter is unusual, the second stanza seeming at first to be constructed in trochaic feet with a sudden conclusion in the stronger iambic form of the first stanza.

```
     //   x/   x(/)
     (x)/  x/   x/
     (x)/  x/   x/   x/
     (x)/  x/   x/
  5  /x   /x   /x
     /x   /x  /(x)
     /x   /x
     /x   xx/  x/
```

The spondee of the first line, along with the pause required by the loss of the final accented syllable in the pattern of the first line and of the initial unaccented syllable in the second line, requires a slowing down, a deliberate retardation, thus matching meter and meaning.

Note too how the nasal sounds of the last stanza (round-chamber-hums-counts-nectars-enters-and-balms) create the "hum" of the bee (along with a suggestion of its buzzing in as-his-hums-his-nectars-enters-is-balms).

I Taste a Liquor Never Brewed (214)

When it first appeared in the *Springfield Daily Republican* (May 4, 1861), this lyric bore the title "The May-Wine." It describes the poet's sense of exhilaration at the magnificence of nature, but in the metaphor of intoxication. The "liquor" which has produced such drunkenness is the air, the dew, summer, the blue of the sky, the bee, the foxglove, the butterfly—the excitable poet, like a child, reels in the wonder of it all. The images flash quickly by, dazzling the reader by their quick succession.

The poet plays the role of the shameless debauchee, apparently evicted from public taverns (the "inns" of heaven's blue) as the bee might be turned out of the blossom whose nectar intoxicates him. Yet she will return to be inebriated again and again by the splendor of the natural world, no matter how much her tippling shocks the observing seraphs and saints (who had, in a sense, renounced the sensual world of nature for the ecstasies of the spirit).

The images are, for all their vividness, exaggerated, as a child would exaggerate them. The closing vision of herself "leaning against the sun" is an awesome hyperbole, one which may indeed be intended to suggest that the intoxication has already taken its toll. The mind becomes alive with a lyric megalomania as the poet "drinks in" the liquor of tangible nature about her.

Except for the trochees at the starts of lines 7, 10, and 16, and the loss of a final syllable in line 15, the meter of the lyric is regular. There are skillful echoings of sound throughout, the alliterations of *t*aste-*t*ankards (lines 1-2), *d*ebauchee-*d*ew (line 6), *b*ee-*b*utterflies (lines 9 and 11), *d*runken-*d*oor-*d*rams-*d*rink (lines 9-12), and *l*ittle-*l*eaning (lines 15-16), topped by the rush of *s*'s in the closing stanza (*s*eraph*s*-*s*wing-*s*nowy-*s*aint*s*-*s*ee-*s*un) (the alliterative effect in this last instance is reinforced too by the other sibilants, such as those at the ends of seraph*s*-hat*s*-saint*s*-window*s*-again*s*t).

Safe in Their Alabaster Chambers (216)

The lyric first appeared in the *Springfield Daily Republican* (March 1, 1862) with the title "The Sleeping." One notes Johnson's presentation of two versions (that of 1859 and that of 1861); however, when the lyric appeared in *Poems* (1890), it was printed as a three-stanza lyric, the second stanza of the version of 1861 attaching itself to the earlier version as a third stanza. It has usually appeared in the three-stanza form in anthologies.

Here is one of Emily Dickinson's most widely praised lyrics on one of her central themes: death and immortality. The dead lie in their cramped houses, surrounded by satin rafters and stone roofs. The breeze laughs gaily above the grave, and the bee whispers its incomprehensible sweet nothings into the flower's stolid earlike shape, and the birds sing their formless, cadenceless songs while centuries pass in the realms of the living. The diadems of kings and Italian magistrates are surrendered to death with as much pomp and ceremonial display as the fall of a snowflake excites.

Yet, while the focus of the images is upon the external and human aspects of death, there is too here the promise of resurrection and immortality—the sleeping victims of mortality awaiting in safety the promise of restored life, all the anxiety of morning and noon, the rush of life, unable to reach them. For all her curiosity about death and her seemingly abnormal obsession with the dying, Miss Dickinson does very often turn her reader's attention to the Christian hope of resurrection and immortality.

The meter of the lyric is unusual, its complexity enlarged by the number of versions and line patterns in which it appeared. Using the two stanzas of the version of 1859 and the second of 1861 as the basis for scansion, we have a scheme like this:

```
      /xx /x   /x   /x
      /xx /x
             x   /xx /(xx)
      /xx /xx x/x /x
  5   /xx /x
             x/   x/

      /xx /
             xx   /xx /x(x)
      /xx /xx /x   /(xx)
 10   /xx /x   /xx /x(x)
      /xx /xx /x   /(xx)

      /xx /xx /xx /x(x)
      /xx /(x)
             x   /xx /(xx)
 15   /xx /x   /xx /x(x)
      /xx /xx /x   /(xx)
```

The poet appears striving for a dactyllic effect, but she arrives at many oddities of arrangement. At times the feet carry over from line to line (e.g., lines 2-3, 5-6, 7-8, 13-14) and require frequent trochaic substitutions (lines 1, 2, 4, 8, 9, 10, 11, 12, 15, and 16).

Phonological interests are a part of the reason for the lyric's success. The sibilant of the opening *safe* stays in the mind from its strong initial position until it is echoed in *sleep* (line 4), *satin* (line 5), and *stone* (line 6). *Sweet* (line 10) and *sagacity* (line 11) keep the effect alive until it comes into full flower in stanza three: crescent (line 12), scoop and arcs (line 13), firmaments (line 14), surrender (line 15), soundless, dots, disc, snow (line 16). Sleep and meek in line 4 provide an arresting example of assonance as do rafter and satin (line 5), laughs (line 7), castle (line 8), and babbles (line 9) later. Of course, the repetition both of word and syntax in lines 2 and 3 and of syntax at other points (*rafter of satin, roof of stone* in stanza one; *laughs the breeze, babbles the bee, pipe the sweet birds* in stanza two; *worlds scoop, firmaments row, diadems drop, doges surrender* in stanza three) give the effect of orderliness in the structure of the lines.

Savior! I've No One Else To Tell (217)

In 1860, the Rev. Charles Wadsworth had visited Emily Dickinson at Amherst. He was then pastor of the Arch Street Presbyterian Church in Philadelphia. It is conjectured that she had met him in 1855 when she had stopped there upon return from Washington. It is usually assumed that his spiritual counsel may have been mistaken for love by her. While a great deal of mystery still surrounds the whole of the interchange (none of the correspondence has survived), it may be safe to assume further that many of her love poems derive from that association.

In April of 1862, Wadsworth was to leave Philadelphia to take the pastorate of Calvary Church in San Francisco, California. If the speculated date of this lyric is correct, Emily may have had some premonition of his departure and have hinted at it here. More generally, the lyric describes the heart burdened down with some- one else's load, with the weight of love which she has borne unful- filled. Now her lover is gone, his heart wrenched from her, but the weight of the aborted love is all the heavier.

She utters the lyric in the form of a prayer, since indeed the whole situation had its potential for great embarrassment, the heart of shy, aging Emily (she was now in her early thirties) taken by a married clergyman sixteen years her elder. She takes note of her own negligence of piety (she grew to dislike the conventionalized religious system of her day, though God was never out of her mind and the Bible was ever her chief inspiration), coming into the presence of God with some embarrassment—she would not have come except in behalf of another, the "imperial heart."

Perhaps the most striking of the phonological effects is that of the repetition of *h* sounds in the last six lines, bringing stress to the words *heavy* and *heavier,* compelling upon the reader the sense of weight and of breathless anxiety in the lines: *heart-had-hold-heart-heavy-heavier.*

While the manuscript copy does not divide the twelve lines into stanzas, they are clearly three stanzas of four lines each, typical alternating tetrameter-trimeter quatrains (common measure) which were Emily Dickinson's most often employed pattern.

The Lamp Burns Sure Within (233)

A discussion of this lyric is included here partly because its compression is a fascination in itself and partly because it gives a good illustration of the sort of laconic understatement common to a number of New England writers. It puzzles us more for what it does not say than by what it does. The central idea expounded is that the flame of the lamp seems utterly oblivious of the labor and aid of those who supply her fuel. The slaves must trim her wick and fill her well with oil, but she burns on oblivious of them all. But she will soon have to reckon with them, for the slave has forgotten to fill the well and has now left. Soon the flame will die, but she is totally unconscious of that threat. The flame has a certain arrogance, a snobbish sense of superiority, refusing to acknowledge her dependence.

At the start of the second stanza there is an interesting compression of syntactic parts. *The lamp* appears to serve a double function as object of *fill* and subject of *burns*. Such is the tendency of this poet, to omit all but the essential, to gain as much through syntactic simplification and compression as possible.

I Like a Look of Agony (241)

First published in *Poems* (1890) with the title "Real" added by her editors, the lyric's theme is love of genuineness, sincerity, authenticity, and, by corollary, dislike of hypocrisy and pretence. The poem itself is an exaggeration, a poetic lie, whose sum is yet a kind of artistic truth. No one "likes" a look of agony; yet one can respect it as issuing from an honest human soul: it does have the look of truth about it. The same may be said of convulsion, of the throe, or of death—there is little hypocrisy in such. Men may sham many other things, but anguish is real, its beads of perspiration a credible testimony.

While the meter here is largely regular (common measure, with only the absence of accented syllables at the ends of lines 3 and 7—a frequent occurrence in Miss Dickinson's quatrains), the rime has the effect of a startling dissonance: *true-throe, feign-strung.* The jar of the poem's theme, its ironical twist (the liking of pain and the look of death) is supported measurably by the harshness of the rime. Here again too the dominance of sibilant sounds adds its cacophony: becau*s*e-it'*s*-*sh*am-convul*s*ion-*s*imulate-eye*s*-glaze-on*c*e-i*s*-impo*ss*ible-bead*s*-angui*sh*-*s*trung. Of the forty words, thirteen have sibilant sounds.

Holding back the tempo at several points in the lyric are passages constructed so as to be difficult to pronounce quickly, their consonants requiring leisure to be sounded: *like a look, men do not sham convulsion, the eyes glaze once, by homely anguish strung.* The pace is retarded by the awkwardness of pronouncing contiguous sounds, especially the clusters of consonants. But the slower pace is essential to the mood and meaning of the lyric.

I've Known a Heaven, Like a Tent (243)

Emily Dickinson here describes the sunset in the simile of the taking down of a circus tent. The stress is not on the dazzling vision, but upon its departure—she captures the sight just as it is disappearing. She adds to the simile of the striking circus that of a bird's disappearance into the horizon—the gay flutter of its oarlike wings and its subsequently being swallowed up by the distance. The uniqueness of the utterance lies in some of the unusual images: for example, the *yards* of the second line may refer to the acres of land on which the circus stands or perhaps to the yards of canvas which make up the tent; the *miles of stare* may suggest the naked landscape when the tent is down or the onlookers standing about gaping at the disassembling. The use of such words as *navigation* (line 14, to suggest the bird's intelligent motion through the sky) and *plash* (line 16, making the sky a splashing sea metaphorically) create a delight in the reading. The tent itself performs its own razing and does not depend upon human agents—it plucks up its own stakes, etc. A slight symbolic hint lingers at the background—the "heaven" perhaps suggesting some bliss or exhilaration which slips away.

Though the lyric is arranged in two stanzas, it actually seems to have been composed in the regular quatrain pattern (lines 11-12 serving together as the third line of stanza three). The rimes are all dissonant except the last (*yards-boards, stare-America* [likely the New England "Ameriker" pronunciation is implied], *yesterday-utterly, hue-view*). The meter moves steadily, though there are clusters of accent which slow down the progress:

```
line 9:        //   //   xx   x/
lines 11-12:   //   //   x
                    /  x/
line 14:       x/   //   x/   x(/)
```

I Can Wade Grief (252)

When it appeared in *Poems* (1891), this lyric was entitled "The Test" by its editors. It presents the ironical paradox that the poet finds it easier to endure pain or grief than joy. The lyric is a marvel of compression, stating its meanings succinctly, enlivening them with metaphor (the pools of grief, the push and intoxication of joy, the strands of strength woven by pain and discipline to create a muscle so powerful that it can hold the weight or burden asked of it). The conclusion is a mythic dramatization of the thesis: give giants balm and it will make weaklings of them; give them a mountain to carry, and they'll shoulder it.

Miss Dickinson has beautifully matched meter to sense in the lyric:

```
     /x   //
     //   xx
     x/   x/
     xx   //   x/
  5  //   x/
     xx   //   x(/)
     (x)/   //   x/
     xx   //   x(/)
     (x)/   x/
 10  /x   x/   x/
     /x   x/   x/
     x/   x/
     //   x/   x(/)
     xx/   x/
 15  x/   x/
     x/   x/
```

The brevity of the lines is kept from fleetness by the number of spondaic feet in the first stanza (lines 1, 2, 4, 6, 7, and 8). The highly erratic rhythm of the last six lines undergirds the semantic evocation of the image of intoxication, the staggering meter matching the stagger of the poet's feet. At the end of line 6 and the start of line 7, as well as at the end of line 8 and the start of line 9, we must either interpolate syllables of pause to fill out the meter or conclude that the two parts of the metrical foot (in each case an iamb) are divided, the first syllable in lines 6 and 8, the second in lines 7 and 9.

There is again a lovely harmony of musical sounds, the *p* sound alliterated in lines 2, 4, and 7, setting the stage for its forceful dominance of line 10. Effective too is the consonantal reversal of *d* and *s* sounds in *stranded* and *discipline* (the *p* sound again carrying an echo of its earlier use). And the *w* sound of *weights* (line 12) and *wilt* (line 14) harks back to the opening verb *wade*, tying first and last together. *Him* (we had anticipated *it*) echoes the first syllable of *Him*maleh (which itself catches the sounds of ba*lm* (line 13) and creates in some ears a suggestion of "They'll carry—Himmaleh!", but avoiding the repetition.

Remarkably, we have usually a distinct sense of rime in the lines, though the matching of sounds is most dissonant: *it-that-feet, smile-all, pain-discipline-hang, men-him.* The sharp frustration of our anticipation in rime aids our comprehension of the poem's irony.

Hope Is the Thing with Feathers (254)

Called "Hope" by its first editors (*Poems,* 1891), this lyric is another of Emily Dickinson's "definition" poems, giving concrete explication and illustration to an abstract term. It is built upon a metaphor in which hope is a bird singing gaily from its perch, through storm, through extremity, and never asking the slightest repayment for its gladdening song. In adversity, it is hope which keeps us from giving in utterly to despair, the unquenchable song of the bird that keeps our souls from fainting. (The one puzzling phrase is that of the third line which may be meant to suggest that the man experiencing "hope" cannot explain why; it is simply a feeling, a "tune" in the soul which warms him unexplainably.)

Significantly, after the imperfect rime of the first stanza, the remaining ones are perfect (stanza two even riming its first and third lines: *heard-bird*). As she frequently does, Miss Dickinson here links line to line by the repetition of a strong consonant sound; the *s* of *s*oul (line 2) is alliterated in *s*ings (line 3), *s*weetest (line 5), *s*ore and *s*torm (line 6), *s*o (line 8), and *s*trangest and *s*ea (line 10). [It is as well repeated internally in such words as sweete*s*t (line 5), mu*s*t (line 6), chille*s*t (line 9), strange*s*t (line 10), e*x*tremity (line 11), and a*s*ked (line 12). Except in the last example, it is always in the sequence of sounds *st*.]

Delight Is as the Flight (257)

Emily Dickinson begins by talking of the swift vanishing of the experience of delight, to end with an elegiac reflection on the swift passage of human life. The opening stanza is elliptical and difficult, perhaps intentionally so to capture the elusiveness of delight. Her description of delight as in the ratio of its flight is meant to suggest that the more intense a delight, the more swiftly it flees and vice versa. So it is with the rainbow, composed as if of brilliant-colored silk—it too flees, its rapturous beauty unable to be sustained.

In the second stanza, the rainbow becomes the symbol of the joys of childhood, a period in the child's life when rainbows dominate, when they are "the common way." But the poetess soon learned how swiftly those excitements could disappear, leaving the sky empty again. The butterfly illustrates the same principle, appearing for a moment, then swiftly gone to be the dower of some distant country-side (note Emily Dickinson's use of the noun *dower* as a verb; such syntactic substitutions are frequent in her verse). And, finally, our lives, having about them that same abrupt transcience, appear a moment and are gone, their "portion" in this "fashion" (i. e., as earthlings) finished.

Emily Dickinson has let the lyric apparently write itself, each line leading to the next, a swift reflection of passing images, yet each bound to the whole by its thesis of transcience (both the transcience of human delight and of human life). Her verse and rime patterns reflect the agitated state of her mind:

```
    x/   x/   x/
    x/   x/   x/   x
    /   x/   x/
    x/   x/
  5 x/
    //   x/   x/
```

```
        x/   x/
        x/   x/
        x/   x/

  10    x/   x/
        x/   x/
        x/   //
        x/   x/   x
        \/   x/
  15    x/   x/
        x/   xx  x/  x/
        x/   x/
        x/   x/   x/

        x/   x/
  20    x/   x/   x/
        //   x/   x/
        x/   x/   x/
        x/   x/   x/  //
        x/   x/
  25    x/   x/   x/   x
        /
```

The first eight lines are couplets, but the ninth does not find its
rime until the fourteenth, the twelfth and thirteenth seeming to have
no rime-mates at all. Line 15 bears the rime of both 17 and 18 (one
perfect, one imperfect), while 17 picks up 19 and 20. The last six
lines pair themselves off as couplets.

Again we see Emily Dickinson's love of the sibilant sounds, the
alliteration of *s* sounds running throughout the lyric: *s*chools, *s*ay
(line 3), *s*kein (line 5), *s*uit (line 7), *s*tripe (line 12), *s*truck (line
13), *s*kies (line 17), *s*o (lines 19-20), *s*een (line 21), *s*ight (line
22), *s*ome, *s*adden (line 24). Other echoes include the *r* and *f*
sounds: *r*atio (line 2), *r*ainbow's (line 4), *r*ain (line 6); *f*right
(line 21), *f*ar (line 23), *f*ashion (line 25). There is as well the
internal rime of line 1, the assonance [*say* (line 3), r*ai*nbow, w*ay*
(line 4), sk*ei*n (line 5), r*ai*n (line 6)] [l*a*st (line 10), *a*sked (line
11)] [wh*en*, b*en*t (line 12), firmam*en*t (line 14), *e*mpty (line 17),
*e*ccentricity (line 18)], and the quaint charm of such pairings as
portion-fashion (line 25) and *stripe-struck up* (lines 12-13), not to
mention the brilliant harmonies of *r, d,* and *n* sounds in the last four
lines.

There's a Certain Slant of Light (258)

One of Emily Dickinson's most widely anthologized poems, the lyric describes her response to a certain moment in nature when a ray of light creates a particular gloom in the winter landscape. The details are atmospheric, the only precise designation being that the light is slant, that it appears in winter, and that it comes as the sun is going toward the west. But its potential is to overpower the poet with its oppressiveness, its capacity to wound the soul, the mind. It is linked in the poet's being with despair, affliction, and death.

The lyric has about it an appropriate mystery, an elusive subjectivity which gives us difficulty in paraphrase. Yet we have all observed the power of the landscape, of an afternoon's gloom, to make us weary or depressed or even exuberant. Miss Dickinson narrows that "mood" to a specific experience recurring for her when the rays of light slant in a particular way on winter afternoons. The nearest she can come to analogy is to say that that slant of light creates in her the same oppressiveness that the music of the cathedral does. Its effect is psychological, spiritual, not physiological. The deathlike atmosphere of a winter afternoon thus forces on the poet the sense of mortality, the consciousness of her own inexorable demise.

The sounds of the lyric are compelling with an abundance of sibilants (both alliterative and consonantal—e. g., certain-*s*lant-oppre*ss*es-*s*car-difference-*s*eal-de*s*pair-*s*ent-land*s*cape-li*s*ten*s*-*sh*adows-di*s*tance-etc.), the use of the *l* sounds at the start (*sl*ant-*l*ight) picked up at the beginning of the fourth stanza (*l*andscape-*l*istens), and the alliterations of *h*eft-*h*eavenly-*h*urt (stanzas one and two) and *d*espair-*d*istance-*d*eath (stanzas three and four), both creating a sense of finality and giving an emphasis to the words in the sequences.

The meter too is oddly irregular, the first three stanzas setting a stanzaic pattern of three trimeter lines followed by a fourth dimeter line. However, the fourth stanza alters the pattern by making its first and third lines tetrameter (the effect is to stretch the lines, to create the sense of breath held or of the look of "distance" in death). There is as well an interesting shift from basically iambic feet in stanzas one and two to basically trochaic feet in stanzas three and four (yet with a final bringing of the lyric to rest on an iambic foot).

$$xx/ \quad x/ \quad x/$$
$$(x)/ \quad x/ \quad x/$$

```
    xx/  x/  x/
    xx/  x/
  5 /x  x/  x/  x
    / x/  //
    xx/  x/  x/
    xx/  x/

    /x  /x  /x
 10 /x  /x  /
    x  x/  x/  x/x
    /x  xx/

    /x  /x  /x  /x
    /x  /x  /(x)
 15 /x  /x  /x  /x
    xx/  x/
```

I Felt a Funeral in My Brain (280)

In the early 1860's, Emily Dickinson was passing through a period of great emotional stress. The Rev. Charles Wadsworth had visited her at Amherst in 1860, and by late 1861 it was clear that he would be leaving Philadelphia soon. The poet suffered through those years such mental anguish as it is difficult to describe; yet it was as well true that 1862 was her most productive year in writing poetry.

The lyric dramatizes in psychological symbol the near mental collapse which the poet suffered in those dreary months of trial. The funeral is itself a metaphor, a construct of the brain, wrought here to convey the deep emotional gloom and despair which the poet now "feels." The sinister beating of the drum (an effect echoed in the steady iambic meter throughout) sounds the "treading-treading" of mourners across her brain and is caught again in the downward dropping of her mind into a kind of insanity.

As the mourners march past the casket, it is as if they are treading upon the poet's soul, her mind growing numb from the monotonous motion of grief. The boots of lead call to mind the "hour of lead" in the later lyric (#341), that hour which follows the experience of great spiritual suffering.

Suddenly the entire universe comes alive with the excruciating tolling of the funeral knell, the poet's entire being reduced to an ear, destined only to hear its shattering sound, silence a strange and alien race unable to rescue her from the shrill ringing of the bells. Madness is her only escape, the benevolence of nature which obliterates the mind so beset with human suffering. "A plank in reason" gave way, setting the poet hurtling downward into the abyss of irrational being, through the chaotic "worlds" of madness.

As I suggested earlier, the lyric is startlingly regular in meter, its stanzas composed of alternating iambic-tetrameter iambic-trimeter lines. It is rescued from monotony altogether by the slow pace imposed upon it, both by pauses required at various points (lines 3, 6, 7, 14, 15) and by the consonant clusters (e.g., line 2: *nd m— rnerst—ndfr*). The predominant sounds are the sibilants (stressed alliteratively throughout: *s*eemed-*s*en*s*e-*s*eated-*s*ervice-*s*oul-*s*ame-*s*pace-*s*ilen*c*e-*s*olitary); they create the unpleasant hissing so appropriate to the mood of despair.

'Tis So Appalling It Exhilarates (281)

The poet's theme is that the terrors of life, once faced and past, lose their horror and take on a fascination. The ambiguity of the word *over* in the second line contains a hint of the idea: such experiences as she describes are "over horror," that is, they go quite beyond horror, they are extreme horrors. However, it is true that only when the horror is "over," ended, does the fascination become a reality. In the security of having experienced the horror and having survived it, the soul stares awe-struck at it. Even death's horror is only in the moment of dying or perhaps as well in the "suspense" of waiting upon it. Anticipation of suffering is the greater trial in it. Once in the throes or beyond them, we find they lose their potency (though the lyric ends equivocally in the oxymoron *gay ghastly,* suggesting that the "liberty" achieved out of the experience's passing is not altogether joyous).

The chief weakness of the lyric lies in its disorganization, a weakness which some may see as a strength, since it is calculated to convey to the reader the poet's bewilderment or confusion of mind in the experiences of "torment." The poem suffers too from an excessive abstractness, its inability to make horror, woe, fright, etc., more than just words.

As in so many of her lyrics upon the subject of human grief, Emily Dickinson here exploits the cacophonous effect of the sibilant sounds: *z, s, sh.* The continued alliterative, assonantal, and consonantal echoings create particularly skillful effects and bind the lines together closely (*so-over-horror-soul*, *horror-half*, *half-captives*, *after-secure-sepulchre-more-stares-fears* in stanza one; *bald-cold-hold* in stanza three; *death-dying*, *death-breath-slumbereth* in stanza four, etc.). The rime is primarily sprung, creating an appropriate dissonance (*secure-more, now-so, sure-prayer, know-now, done-come, liberty-free-holiday*). The meter and stanzaic patterns are halting and, at times, disjointed, thus undergirding the lyric's semantic sense of disorder and turmoil.

The Robin's My Criterion for Tune (285)

We are what our environment has made us; we judge all from our own limited, provincial viewpoints, forgetting that others may view the world about them from equally idiosyncratic eyes. Emily Dickinson is a native New Englander and thus sees life "New Englandly," favoring robin and buttercup and snow in winter. But everyone else judges by equally subjective standards. There is a touch both of pride and self-confidence in the lines, the poet unwilling to see the world in any other way, adopting a regal posture at the conclusion of the lyric to confirm her sovereignty in judgment.

While the underlying meter is iambic throughout, the lines of the poem vary in length from two to five feet, the opening four lines growing foot by foot shorter (pentameter, tetrameter, trimeter, dimeter). Lines 5-9 follow a similar pattern of progressive shortening of line length, but the four- and three-foot patterns are repeated (tetrameter, tetrameter, trimeter, trimeter, dimeter). Line 10 is tetrameter again, 11-14 trimeter, 15-17 again shortening tetrameter, trimeter, dimeter. This pattern of progressively shortening lines, in effect a failure to meet the reader's expectation of length, gives a note of finality to the statement (almost as if the poet says, I refuse to say more, to satisfy your expectation for one or two more feet).

The rimes too have about them a quality of defiance: *tune-noon-bloom* suggest, but do not really echo one another with perfect harmony; similarly, *born-spurn* and *fit-it-taught* set the ears slightly ajar by their mild dissonance.

A Clock Stopped (287)

Emily Dickinson describes death in the metaphor of the stopped clock. This marker of the hours in time can no longer govern the life of the deceased—and no "shopman's" skill can restore the ticking of the still heart. Switzerland, the great center of clockmaking, has no craftsman so skilled as can put to order again the fragile mechanism of the human life that has left the measured sphere of time to dwell in everlasting day. The physician strives to revive the heartbeat, the cold motionless pendulum of the corpse, but the dead arrogantly resist the skilled efforts of restoration (a striking hyperbole).

The lyric has a remarkable regularity metrically, with only infrequent substitutions to avoid the disastrous monotony of perfect scansion. The first lines, as well as the last two, are in reality one (in each case a trimeter line). The elided feet at the ends of lines 4, 6, 10, 12, and 14, create necessary pauses, holding the lyric back momentarily, allowing the second's reflection needed for comprehension.

```
        x/   /
             /   x/x
        x/  x/  x/
        //  x/  x/  x(/)
    5   x/  //  x/

        x/  x/  x/  x(/)
        x/  x/  x/
        x/  x/  x/  x/
        x/  x/  x/

    10  x/  x/  x/  x(/)
        x/  x/  x/
        x/  x/  x/  x(/)
        x/  x/  x/

        /x  x/  x/  x(/)
    15  /x  x/  x/
        /x  x/  x/  x/
        x/  x/
                x/
```

The three trochaic line openings of the last stanza suggest the erratic nod of the corpse, resisting the physician's skill.

As in most of her lyrics, Emily Dickinson here weaves an intricate fabric of echoed sounds (clock-stopped-not, lines 1-2; can't-put-puppet, line 4; decimals-degreeless-doctors-decades-dial, lines 8-10, 16-17; cool-concernless, line 13; no-nods-nods, lines 13-15; seconds-slim, line 15; dial-life, line 17).

I'm Nobody! Who Are You? (288)

One of Emily Dickinson's most playful lyrics (published originally with the title "Nobody"), these two brief stanzas nonetheless bespeak the poet's shyness and withdrawal, her desire to retreat from the public affairs of life, her contentment with an existence without fame or continual human contact. Yet the lyric has a note of irony in its theme—"nobody's" great delight at finding another "nobody," a companion for her negative being (whether she has specific reference to an acquaintance, her sister-in-law Sue or the Rev. Wadsworth, for example, or whether she had indeed seen the lyric "Little Nobody" in the *Springfield Daily Republican* [January 23, 1858] is not clear).

The poem's charm is in its simplicity, the intentionally naive exaggeration of the threat of publicity, the amusingly effective simile of the noisy frog, celebrating its own importance with a forthright pride. The metric starts and stops, particularly in stanza one, supporting the excitement of the discovery as well as the stealth of its revelation:

```
  //   xx   (x)/   x/
  x/   /x   x/
  x/   x/   x/
  //   //   x/   x/
5 //   xx   x/   xx
  //   x/   x/
  x/   x/   x/   //
  xx   x/   x/
```

(One suspects the first foot of line four is actually the final foot of line three, giving the lyric a more regular alternating tetrameter-trimeter arrangement.)

I Know Some Lonely Houses off the Road (289)

When it first appeared in *Poems* (1890), the lyric was entitled by its editors "The Lonely House." It is atmospheric, creating the shimmering vision of a lonely house on a back road, easy prey to robbers, its muffled sounds of antique clock and quiet mice moving upon the scene. The objects about the house come alive—the walls, spectacles, the almanac, the mat—the eerie light of the moon casting its magic

upon them. In the morning, when the rooster cries for his rafter, the
elderly inhabitants rise to find the door still open, as yet unconscious
of their stealthy visitors of the night.

The lyric is intricately wrought both in meter and poetic device.
The lines vary from monometer to pentameter, the rimes weaving
in and out (sometimes perfect, but more often sprung) in irregular
patterns. Were it not for the firm iambic pattern undergirding the
whole, the lyric might seem to have been written in free verse.

	pentameter	x/	x/	x/	x/	x/	a
	pentameter	x/	x/	x/	x		b
						/ x/	a
	pentameter	x/	x/	x/			c
5					x/	x/	c
	tetrameter	x/	x/				c
				x/	x/		d
	tetrameter	//	x/				e
				x/	x/		d
10	trimeter	x/	//	x/			d
	dimeter	//	x/				e
	trimeter	x/	x/	x/			e
		//	x/	x/	x/	x/	a
		x/	x/				b
15		x/	x/	x/			b
		x/	x/				c
		x/	x/	//			d
		//					d
		x/	x/	x/	x/	x/	a
20		x/	x/	x/			a
		/x	x/	/			b
				x	x/	x/	a
		x/	//	x/			a
		x/	//				a ⎤
25		x/	x/				a ⎦
		/x	x/				b
		/x	x/				b
		x/	//	x/			c
		x/	x/	x/			d

```
30                        // x/                          a⎤
                          // x/                          a⎥
                          //                             a⎥
                          x/ x/ x/                       b⎦
                          xx // x/                       b
35                        // x/                          b
                          //                             b⎤
                          x/ x/ x/                       a⎥
                          //                             b⎦
                          xx // x/ x/                    b
40                        /x x/ x/ x/ x/                 b
```

I Got So I Could Take His Name (293)

Here is another of the frequent love lyrics which Emily Dickinson wrote in the early 1860's, likely out of her infatuation for Rev. Charles Wadsworth, the clergyman whom she had met in Philadelphia in 1855 and who helped her through the spiritual crisis she had been suffering. Wadsworth had visited the poet a year earlier (in 1860), and she, though conscious that her love for him could never culminate in marriage, wrestles with the difficulty of forgetting him. She is now at the point of mastery—she can hear his name uttered at last without its devastations upon her soul.

One of the chief devices of the lyric is hyperbole—the soul (or heartbeat?) stopped at hearing his name uttered, the thunder, the rending of sinews, the staples driven through the chest (to impede breathing). Yet the exaggeration is balanced by the lyric understatement: at last she has learned to bring her grief to God, though she can dimly recall Him (the face of her lover, an "ordained" clergyman, who ought to have pointed her thought to God, has instead driven God from her very recollection). Her grief is so enormous that her faith has been shaken, God shrinking to a dim memory. She can address her petition only to the cloud, not certain whether indeed Deity stands behind it or whether, if He does, He could care, in His remoteness, for the insignificance of her love (though to her it is a vast and overwhelming misery).

The first three stanzas (each starting with *I got so I could . . .* , a phrase suggested again at the start of the fourth stanza in the single word *could*) dramatize her gain of control: now she can hear his name, walk where he stood, look through his letters, all without the devastation of soul she had at first experienced. The last three

half contradict the first three, revealing again the pitiful condition
of the spirit which longs to ask the help of God, but which, in its
despair, can scarcely muster the faith to do so.

It is notable how the poet gives the quality of speech to the entire
lyric: the self-interruption of the second line, added to the implied
gesturing and assuming of a posture in line seven, gives a note of in-
formality to the whole, a sense supported too by the irregular metric
of the last stanza:

```
//   xx   x/
x/   x/   x/   x/
//   xx   x/
x/   x/   x/   x/
x/   x/   x/
x/   xx
x/   //   x/   x/   x/
```

Yet, as in much of her poetry, Emily Dickinson evidences here
the great care for sound, the interest in subtly imperfect rimes, in
echoes of vowel and consonant. Note, for example, the rime of *name*
and *gain* in stanza one, paired off again in the consonantal rime of
name and *room,* the dissonance of *God* and *failed* in stanza four, as
well as that of *despair-affair-more* in the last stanza. We have come
to expect the sibilant alliteration (*s*top-*s*ensation-*s*oul-*s*inew-*s*tir-*s*ta-
ples), the echoings of th*at-a*ngle (line 6), *t*urned-*t*urned-*t*ore (lines
7-8), *c*ould-re*c*ollect-*c*all (lines 13-14), *f*ormula-*f*ailed (line 16),
*mi*nute-*mi*sery-*mo*re (lines 25-27).

(Note that by stricter arrangement the lyric can actually be shown
to contain five quatrains and a sixth sestet, built generally on the patterns of common measure [alternating iambic tetrameters and trim-
eters]. As it stands, line 18 contains the last two feet of line 17, line
21 ends quatrain five. The sestet starts at line 22, the last two lines
actually suggesting:

As misery. Itself too vast
For interrupting more.

The stanzaic pattern is thus much more regular than as it appeared
in the original packet.)

Your Riches Taught Me Poverty (299)

Some have urged that this lyric is a "memorial" poem, commemo-
rating the death of Ben Newton some nine years earlier. He had en-

tered the poet's life in 1847 when he worked as an apprentice in her father's law office. He had first awakened her mind to literature, having given her copies of the Bronte novels and of Emerson. His death in 1853 of consumption cost Emily Dickinson dearly.

There is in the lyric a reminiscence of Keats' "On First Looking into Chapman's Homer," both poets startled by the immense treasure to be seen upon entering a new literary experience (for Keats, the discovery of Homer in Chapman's translation; for Emily Dickinson, the rich friendship with Ben Newton). The poet had thought herself wealthy (a millionaire) until she met Newton. The youth (he was 27, Emily only 17, a girl at school) was, as the hyperbole suggests, whole new realms (metaphorically her Buenos Aires, her Peru). She had had only the meagerest knowledge of "gems" (enough to have been impressed by the queen's jewels) until she met Newton—his great personal "wealth" had made her seem a beggar (Golconda was the rich diamond-cutting city of India in the sixteenth century). Yet the treasure was not hers to keep—she had ascertained it only as it departed—only when Newton left Amherst and, within three years, died, only then could the poet see the genuine worth of that treasure, the gold and pearl of Newton's intellectual and artistic gifts.

The meter of the lyric is again regular (with occasional pauses at the ends of iambic tetrameter lines: 5 and 21), the rimes conventional (except *deem-gem* of stanza six and the unusual *pearl-girl-school* of stanza eight). Alliteration is again the chief device of sound (*m*yself-*m*illionaire, *b*oast-*b*road-*B*uenos, *d*rifted-*d*ominions-*d*ifferent, *P*eru-*p*overty, *c*olors-*c*ommonest, etc.).

I Reason, Earth Is Short (301)

Emily Dickinson presents here the antithesis of a consolation of philosophy. Reasoning in each stanza to a philosophical "answer" to the frustrations of finiteness, she rejects each by saying in effect—so what? The answers are those frequently heard—life is short; everyone has his share of suffering; you don't have to live; all will be set right in heaven. Yet none of these solutions can satisfy the troubled spirit of the poet. She leaves the reader to share in her own bewilderment.

It is important to remember that, at this point in her life, Emily Dickinson is suffering a great emotional crisis, a period of strain which blighted her entire experience, yet one which had resulted also in her greatest artistic output (she produced more poems during 1862 than in any other year). She had never really accepted the death of Ben Newton or the departure of Wadsworth to California. In desperation, she had written to Col. Higginson, asking his appraisal of her lyric gift. While never quite understanding her poetry, he encouraged her. The correspondence continued until her death.

One of the remarkable things about the lyric is its quick, emphatic manner of dealing with each point of reason. The effect is achieved largely in the abrupt trimeter and dimeter lines, the two-foot utterance at the end of each stanza ("But what of that?"), made all the more startling by the trimeter lines which precede them. The finality of her refusal to accept the consolatory alternatives cannot be mistaken. Note too the near defiance in the tone created by the last line's disagreement with the rimes of the stanzas (though all the rimes are dissonant: *short-absolute-hurt; die-vitality-decay; heaven-even-given*).

The Soul Selects Her Own Society (303)

When it first appeared in *Poems* (1890), the editors had entitled this lyric "Exclusion." Its theme is the determined autocracy of the human soul, selecting its companions and rejecting all those it wishes to exclude. As in a number of her lyrics, the poet first states her argument absolutely, only to dramatize it in the subsequent stanzas. The chariots of nobility, even that of an emperor, seek admission into the soul's privacy, but, no matter how lowly that soul, it remains obdurate in its selection. Like God, she is a majority of one—her soul's vote cast against a man, he can gain no admission.

The determination of the soul's unilateral action is supported in the lyric by the brief, emphatic verses which alternate with the longer (except in the case of line 1, tetrameter) verses. In the last stanza, lines 2 and 4 are spondaic, creating a distinct impression that the poet has stomped her foot in determination—her decision is final.

The final stanza brings together too the poetic figures of hyperbole, metaphor, and simile. The exaggeration of the "nation" of callers seeking to gain entry contrasts securely with the "one" that she has selected. The closed valves (calling to the mind the center of her being, the seclusive heart), mixed in figure with the "stony" resistance of the soul, bring the lyric to emphatic end.

Quite naturally the lyric has been thought of peculiar significance as the product of a spirit reclusive by nature. Emily Dickinson's continual refusal to mingle socially at Amherst, her selection of the small world of acquaintances ("seen" mainly in her letters to and from them), creates in the reader's mind a clear sense of self-analysis in the lyric.

The Difference Between Despair (305)

Emily Dickinson wrote a good many lyrics which are efforts at definition. Here she distinguishes between synonyms (though certainly not very close synonyms), despair and fear. It is a lyric associated with her personal emotional crisis, an analogical description of despair. Fear is like the moment of catastrophe, the sudden terror of impact; despair is like the memory of it, the mind without agitation, motionless, paradoxically looking and not seeing, locked within its own being, and content (if such can be). The rigid inactivity of the despairing soul is likened to the sculptured bust, frozen into incomprehension of life about it.

The rimes are dissonant (*one-been, eye-see*), the internal echoes setting up jarring half-rimes (*despair-fear, one-between-instant*). The sibilants appear again, along with alliterative (*d*ifference-*d*espair, *m*ind-*m*otion) and assonantal (wr*e*ck-wh*e*n-wr*e*ck-b*ee*n) effects.

The Soul's Superior Instants (306)

The lyric's theme—the moments of spiritual insight which the soul sometimes achieves in solitude—turns our attentions in the end to one of Emily Dickinson's obsessions: immortality. The individual soul has moments when it shares in the eternal, moments of solitude (when all activity has ceased and every mortal friend has withdrawn), moments when it rises above mortality (through experience), when it views, apparition-like, the significance of immortality (the colossal *substance* of what is altogether intangible to flesh and comprehensible only to spirit).

The lyric requires time for its signification to be assimilated. Emily Dickinson thus slows it down by the implied pauses required by the meter at the ends of lines:

```
x/   x/   xx/   x(/)
x/   x/   x/
x/   x/   x/   x(/)
x/   x/   x/
```

```
 5   x/   x/   x/   x(/)
     x/   x/   x/
     x/   x/   x/   x(/)
     x/   x/   x/

     x/   x/   x/   x(/)
10   x/   x(caesura)/   x/
     x/   x/   x/   x(/)
     x/   x/   x/

     x/   x/   x/   x(/)
     x/   x/   x/
15   xx   x/   x/   x(/)
     x/   x/   x/
```

Without the enforced pauses, the reflective breaks in pattern, the lyric's sing-song would be deadening. As it stands, however, they provide the slight hesitation needed for comprehension of the whole.

The music of the lyric, its alliterations (*soul's-superior, remote-recognition, favorites-few*), internal rimes (*occur-to her, when-friend*), dissonant end rimes (*alone-withdrawn, height-omnipotent, few-immortality*), its consonances (*instants-alone-when-friend-and-infinite-withdrawn, favorites-colossal-substance*), shows it carefully wrought, an example of the skill which Miss Dickinson so frequently displays in her juggling with sounds.

He Fumbles at Your Soul (315)

When it first appeared in *Poems* (1896), the lyric was entitled "The Master" by its editors. That title suggests that the lyric depicts the soul in the grip of God, who first fumbles at it in preparation for the great calamity, the spiritual anguish which He finally intends for it. He is like a pianist, feeling about the keyboard to be sure He is ready, that He is in full control of His instrument (His performance suggests a different kind of mastery). He gives the soul a chance to accustom itself to the initial fumbling, preparing it for the stunning blow which lies just ahead, the blows of the hammers heard faintly in the distance. The soul has its premonitions: it knows that the *coup de grâce,* the final crushing blow, is about to be delivered. It stiffens in anticipation, hesitates a moment until the thundrous stroke is felt, the soul left naked and bleeding (as an Indian warrior leaves his scalped victim). The final analogy—that of the forest stripped by tornadic winds—suggests the moment of calm which just precedes calamity, the soul's certainty that the blow is to come.

Miss Dickinson's use of metaphor is unusual here. Human nature, the soul, lacking physical substance, is nonetheless "brittle," while the hammers of calamity are "ethereal," without material presence as well. The breath, a metonymy for life, is like the body as it stiffens before the hammer's blow. God, like the pagan Zeus, strikes in the thunderbolt, the natural "messenger" of heaven, bringing its assurance of the potential fury of the skies.

The lyric is composed largely in the short meter of the hymn (lines 1, 2, and 4 of each stanza are iambic trimeter; line 3 iambic tetrameter). It appears there are three quatrains with a fourth incomplete one (she may have intended to return later to write a first and second line for the last stanza):

```
      x/   x/   x/
      x/   x/   x/
      x/   x/   //  x/
      x/   x/   x/
  5   x/   x/   x/x
      xx   x/   x/
      x/   x/   x/  x/
      x/   x/   //
      x/   x/   x/x
 10   x/   x/   x/
      //   x/   x/  x/
      x/   x/   x/
      (?)
      (?)
      x/   x/   x/  x/
      x/   x/   x/
```

I'll Tell You How the Sun Rose (318)

Entitled "A Day" by its editors when it first appeared in *Poems* (1890), the lyric does describe in metaphor both dawn and dusk. The poet scarcely notices the sun itself emerging over the horizon, but she observes its effects on the landscape, the ribbons of light, the tall steeples losing their grayish darkness in the radiant purple of dawn, the startled hills, receiving the swift spreading news, untying their bonnets, like maidens, as if to let their hair down and to participate in the gaity, the birds beginning their bright morning songs. Surprised by the newly enlivened landscape, the poet recognizes that the sun must have risen.

The setting of the sun is described in quite a contrasting mood—a fairy tale world of golden children ascending the purple stile of heaven, received by the gray-frocked friar of evening who leads them like sheep to their rest, closing the gate of night after him.

The lyric's strength lies in the vividness of its metaphors, the concrete way in which it dramatizes dawn and dusk, in addition to its alliterative music (*r*ose-*r*ibbon-*r*an, *s*un-*s*teeples-*s*wam-*s*quirrels-*s*aid-*s*oftly-*s*un-*s*et-*s*eemed-*s*tile, *b*onnets-*b*obolinks-*b*egun).

Of All the Sounds Despatched Abroad (321)

When Thomas Wentworth Higginson used this lyric in an article he had contributed to *The Christian Union* (XLII, September 25, 1890), he entitled it "The Wind." It expresses the poet's delight in the mysterious music of the wind, singing its free, exhilarating song as it rushes through the trees. It is as if the heavens were an Aeolian harp upon which the fingers of the wind play, filling the air with music. Such a treasure, an inheritance, can never be earned or, once experienced, stolen by robbers. It is an inward, spiritual wealth, carried with us throughout our days upon earth and, possibly, taken even to the grave. Perhaps there the dust of the dead dance merrily to the wind's tune, celebrating some strange holiday in the delight of bird and wind. How sad, should there be one soul so miserable as never to have heard the wind's chant, the full and radiant harmony of that music.

The lyric is composed in three eight-line stanzas and a fourth nine-line stanza. (However, its conception is actually that of eight quatrains, each in common measure; lines 31 and 32 together make up the last iambic tetrameter of the eighth quatrain. Emily Dickinson was not always careful about the arrangements of lines and stanzas in her written drafts of the lyrics. Unfortunately, the publication of them without editorial correction can mislead the reader newly come to her poetry.)

In her lyric reflection upon the wind's melody, she maintains a fairly strict metrical pattern [even resorting at times to awkward syntax to maintain the rhythm: note, for example, her use of the active for the passive infinitives in lines 10 and 11—"to (be) earn(ed)," "to (be) take(n) away"]. But the interweaving of sounds is remarkable (note the echo of "wind" in "working" and "hand," line 5; of "fingers" in "inner," lines 13-14; of "golden" in "whole" and "days," line 15; of "even" in "in" and "urn," line 16; of "winds" in "round" and "bands," line 21, etc.). Alliteration (*m*easure-*m*elody, *c*omb-*qu*iver, *t*ufts-*t*une, *g*ain-*g*otten-*g*olden, *b*ands-*b*irds-*b*ear, *s*ky-*s*wept-*s*eamless) and assonance (w*i*nd-f*i*ngers-qu*i*ver-w*i*th-per-m*i*tted, tr*ai*t-t*a*ke-*a*way-g*ai*n, g*o*tten-*no*t, b*o*ne-g*o*lden-wh*o*le, cr*a*ve-gr*a*ce) again play major roles.

There Came a Day at Summer's Full (322)

When it appeared in *Scribner's Magazine* (VII, August 1890), the lyric had been entitled "Renunciation." In 1860, Wadsworth had visited Emily Dickinson at Amherst. It is possible she describes here that perfect day of their meeting, he a pastor who had encouraged her writing of poetry and had helped her through a time of sore spiritual distress, she a shy and devoted child who had mistaken his concern over her turmoil for love.

The poet describes that day in sacramental terms, so firmly does it remind her of the bliss of heaven, and days following resurrection when the soul is at one with Christ. Yet the sun marks out its temporal hours, the flowers blossom in seasonal beauty—it is summer. The lovers scarcely spoke, there was no need. Their sense of love's sympathy was as great as that of the communicant at his Lord's table, rehearsing for the marriage supper of the Lamb of God (marriage is a basic Christian symbol, the church portrayed metaphorically as the bride of Christ).

Time slips away swiftly; the lovers part, the image of the parting ships dramatizing metaphorically the reluctance of farewell. The separating lovers swear each by the other's crucifixes, their loves bound until the morning of resurrection (the repetition of this image, the same as that at the end of the first stanza, brings us back to the initial scene), when death will lie defeated, their lives intertwined again in the eternal marriage of heaven, the Calvaries of love suggesting the anguish of the parting lovers which will finally justify them in their clandestine relationship.

The stanzaic pattern is the common measure which Emily Dickinson had learned in reading the New England hymnal ("this time" at the end of line 14 actually belongs at the start of line 15, and "Justified" at the start of line 28 belongs at the end of line 27). The rimes begin perfectly, matching the radiance of the summer day, but by stanza three they are imperfect, hinting at the lovers' enforced separation (*word-Lord,* a common hymnal rime; *time-Lamb; sound-bond; grave-love,* an ironic echo perhaps intended to suggest the reality that the lovers must take their love to the grave with them).

Here can be seen samples of Miss Dickinson's skill at lyric compression: for example, the "as common" of line 5 compresses some such structure as "as (it was) common (for it to do)"; the "accustomed" of line 6 stands for "(as they were) accustomed (to do)." Here too is demonstrated her unusual skill in alliteration (*s*ummer's-*s*aints-*s*un-*s*oul-*s*olstice-*s*carce-*s*peech-*s*ymbol-*s*acrament-*s*ealed-*s*upper-*s*lid, *w*ord-*w*as-*w*ardrobe, *b*ack-*b*ound-*b*ound-*b*ond), assonance (*ca*me-*da*y, *ea*ch-*ea*ch-*sea*led, *sou*nd-*bou*nd), and consonance (*com*mon-ac*cus*tomed, a*b*road-*b*lew, *sol*stice-pa*ss*ed, *com*mune-*tim*e, de*ck*s-loo*k*-ba*ck*).

Some Keep the Sabbath Going to Church (324)

The lyric first appeared in the weekly review *The Round Table* (March 1864) with the title "My Sabbath," though it was later published in *Poems* (1890) with the title "A Service of Song." The poet expresses her dislike for the formalized services of the church, her preference for the quiet reverence of nature. She had angered her father on a number of occasions by her refusal to attend services with the family. She found the ostentation and elaborateness of public worship offensive.

"At home" she conducts her own "service," listening to the "choir" of migratory songbirds, awed by the orchard's "dome." In the open cathedral of nature, the poet hears the voice of God in quiet meditation (note the litotes of God as a clergyman delivering no long-winded discourse, but communicating the very reality of heaven in a short and simple sermon). She is already seated in the heavenlies, already in the presence of her God, not in the intermediary bosom of the church.

While the lyric is simple in meaning, it is more subtle and complex in meter, built upon the pattern of alternating tetrameters and trimeters:

```
    //  x/  x/  xx/
    //  x/  xx/
   xx/  x/  xx/  x/
   xx/  x/  x/

 5  //  x/  xx/  x(/)
   (x)/  x/  x/
   xx/  x/  xx/  x/
    x/  x/  x/

    //  xx/  x/  x/
10 xx/ xx/  x/
   xx/  x/  xx/  xx/
    x/  x/  x/
```

The spondees at the starts of the first two stanzas stress the contrast between *some* and *I*. That at the start of the third stanza reinforces the startling effect of her identification of the presiding clergyman—God. The frequent substitutions of anapestic for iambic feet convey the sense of sprightliness of elation, which the poet feels in her "service." There is not the oppressive tone of the cathedral, but the lightness of the spirit liberated in nature.

The rimes of the first two stanzas are perfect, that of the third a mere repetition (*long, -long*). The *home-dome* of stanza one picks up the *some* (of both stanzas one and two), both as a consonantal (*m* sound) and sight (*-ome*) rime. Again we observe the fascination of sibilants for the poet (*some-sabbath-staying-surplice-sexton-sings-sermon*; note the significance of each of these words in the total meaning—a resting of emphasis partly in the repetition of the sound). There are other repetitions as well: c*horister-or*chard (lines 3-4); *wear-wings* (line 6); *tolling-bell-little* (lines 7-8); c*lergyman-sermon* (lines 9-10); *God-getting-going* (lines 9, 11-12).

Of Tribulation, These Are They (325)

First printed in Higginson's *Atlantic Monthly* article (LXVIII, October 1891) with the title "The Saint's Rest," and later in *Poems* (1891) with the title "Saved!", the lyric takes its opening words from Revelation VII:14. The Apostle John, in his vision of the great tribulation to come upon the earth, sees a multitude of Gentiles standing before the throne of God in white robes and with palm leaves in their hands. When John asks who these hosts are, an elder answers: "These are they which came out of great tribulation and have washed their robes and have made them white in the blood of the Lamb."

As the poet describes these "tribulation" saints, she contrasts them with others wearing "spangled gowns, a lesser rank / Of victors," lesser because their arrival had been relatively easy, had not led them through martyrdom. The tribulation "saints are designated" by the simple snow-white, unornamented robe (the emblem of their salvation—their garments washed in the Lamb's blood) and the palm branch (the symbol of their martyrdom). These are the "superior" souls who have never surrendered even though in the anguish of defeat driven into hiding, forced to travel the roads at night when their "panting" ankles could scarcely carry them. They have come at last to the house of God, having been brought through trial to the eternal bliss of heaven.

The meter of the lyric is largely regular (note that "But the ones" is actually part of the tetrameter of line 5, and should be included there in the scansion:

line 5:   // x/ x↓
line 6:   / x/ x/ x/ //).

An accented syllable is missing at the end of line 11, a common effect in the Dickinson method; the accent is to be taken in pause:

line 11: x/ x/ x/ x(/).

There are a number of spondaic substitutions, each of which aids the semantic emphasis of the words (e. g., *all these,* line 5; *most times,* line 6; *wear-noth-,* line 7; *no or-,* line 8).

There appear too several echoes of sound: *these* (lines 1 and 5), *d*enoted-*d*esignate (lines 2 and 4), s*now-no* (lines 7-8), *conquer-commoner* (lines 5 and 7), *p*anting-*a*nkle-*p*assed (line 13), and *we said-was saved* (line 16). Note too the cluster of sibilants at the start of stanza three (*s*urrender-i*s-s*ort-thi*s-s*uperior-*s*oil).

I Cannot Dance Upon My Toes (326)

By negation the poet sets the basic metaphor of the lyric: that of the dance within the mind. Her body cannot move in the graceful rhythm of dance, but her mind does. Had she studied ballet, she might have been able to express her glee in the exhilaration of the pirouette, dazzling her audiences by the grace and charm of her performance, causing the prima ballerina to turn white with envy as she wheels and soars in her rich eider-down costume, hearing from the wings the applause of her delighted spectators. Yet apart from the world of her soul's fancy, in the reality of her plainer existence, no one has any hint of her mind's dancing, of her mind as alive with its own ballet as is the opera house with the actual spectacle.

To match the remarkable metaphorical utterance, Miss Dickinson played upon sound and meter in an equally intricate performance. The repetition of the first stanza (*me-me*) and the imperfect rimes of the second (*abroad-mad*) and last stanzas (*here-opera,* despite the New England pronunciation of the word) suggest the discrepancy of mind and body, of the exotic motion of the soul's ballet as set against the clumsy movement of the body (*hopped, claw,* and *tossed* may be meant to suggest the physical awkwardness of the poet).

Note especially the echoings of alliteration (*b*allet-*b*lanch and *p*irouette-*p*rima in stanza two; *g*own-*g*auze and *h*air-*h*opped in stanza three; *s*now-*s*ight-*s*ound-*s*o in stanza four; *n*or-*kn*ow-*kn*ow in stanza five), assonance (c*a*nnot-d*a*nce-m*a*n in stanza one; the internal rime of *gl*ee-*m*e in line four; *ou*t-s*ou*nd-h*ou*se in stanza four), and consonance (a*m*ong-*m*y-*m*ind in stanza one; ba*ll*s-ro*ll*ed-whe*el*s-ti*ll* in stanza four).

Before I Got My Eye Put Out (327)

First published in *Poems* (1891) with the title "Sight," the lyric refers to the eye affliction which took Emily Dickinson to Boston several times in 1864 and 1865. After that time, however, the malady seems to have been cured, for reference to it does not recur. The poem is, nonetheless, a pose, since the poet claims utter blindness, one so profound that she cannot see at all the sensuous beauty of life about her. Instead, she looks with her soul pressed against the window pane, guessing what sky, meadows, mountains, forests, stars, etc., are like. Physical sight had delighted her as much as it had any mortal, but, having lived in darkness, she doesn't think her soul could bear sight again; her heart could not endure such exhilaration.

There is an interesting ambiguity in the last stanza arising from the ellipsis: one does not know whether the poet means "so (it is) safer (only to) guess (what these natural objects look like)" or "so (it is) safer, (I) guess, (to stand here) with just my soul upon the window pane." She does create both possibilities by her elliptical method.

The lyric is again relatively regular in its alternating iambic tetrameters, iambic trimeters (lines 9 and 10 are actually a single iambic tetrameter line: x/ x/ — x/ x/). The rimes create a dissonance suitable to the strange denial of the desire for sight (*see-way, sky-me, stars-eyes, road-dead, pane-sun*). The use of assonance (*I-eye*-my-*I*-liked in stanza one; *I*-my-fini*te*-*eye*s in stanza three), alliteration (*told-to-today, might-mine-meadow-mountains* and *sky-split-size* in stanzas two and three; *motions-morning's-mine* and *look-liked* in stanza four; *so-safer-soul-sun* in stanza five), and consonance (*as-creatures-eyes* in stanza one; *mountains-meadows-stars-eyes* and *forests-stintless-stars* in stanza three).

A Bird Came Down the Walk (328)

When collected in *Poems* (1891), this lyric was entitled by its editors "In the Garden." Like so many others, it reveals her love of "nature's people," her delight in the behavior of a bird. She catches him when he is not aware of her: he lunches upon an angleworm, satisfies his thirst by partaking of the grass's dew (note the inevitable suggestion of the word *glass* from the semantic clue of drinking and the riming hint of *grass-glass*). In a few deft details she presents his character: the hopping, the frightened, rapid glance of the eyes, the stirring velvet head, the distrustful nature.

The poet approaches cautiously with a "crumb" (note the ambiguity of the adjective *cautious;* it seems to modify both poet and bird), frightening her reluctant guest. The bird takes flight, feathers unfurled, rowing confidently through the ocean of air (the metaphor of ocean-air brings with it the lovely closing image of the butterflies leaping from the banks into the pool of atmosphere). There appears in the word *softer* a characteristic instance of syntactic ambiguity: *softer* is an adjective, but it appears to modify *rowed*, suggesting it functions as an adverb. Actually the poet achieves a double effect: the adjective reflects upon the bird's softness, the adverb upon the softness of the rowing.

Miss Dickinson gives us perfect rimes in the opening two stanzas (*saw-raw, grass-pass*) perhaps to suggest the tranquillity of the situation, but she shifts to dissonant rime in the last three stanzas (*around-*

head, crumb-home, seam-swim) perhaps to suggest the agitation of the bird as it quickly soars to its escape.

The meter is fairly regular, the lyric built upon the short measure pattern, the third line of each stanza iambic tetrameter to avoid the potential monotony of the other three short iambic trimeter lines. However, the last two stanzas depart slightly from our expectation:

```
IV   x/   x/   x/x
     x/   x/   x/
     x/   x/   x/   x(/)
     x/   x/   x/

V    x/   x/   x/x
     //   xx   x/
     x/   x/   x/   x/
     //   xx   x/
```

The phonetic echoes are not so abundant as in some of Miss Dickinson's lyrics, though *d*rank-*d*ew (line 5), side*w*ise-*w*all (line 7), *gl*anced-*r*apid (line 9), *c*autious-*c*rumb (lines 13-14), un*r*olled-*r*owed-home (lines 15-16), *oa*rs-*o*cean (line 17), *s*ilver-*s*eam (line 18), and *b*utterflies-*b*anks (line 19) create interesting effects. Also, the tongue twisting *leap-plashless* (line 20) has a fascination of its own.

The Grass So Little Has To Do (333)

When it appeared in *Poems* (1890), the lyric had been entitled "The Grass" by its editors. Envying the leisurely, simple, and beautiful life of the grass in its progress from field to loft, the poet longs to exchange her more complicated life for that of the lowly plant's. The simplicity of the grass's activities is the first invitation—it has so little to do: a few butterflies and bees to look after (note the ambiguity of *brood,* suggesting both the hatching of the butterfly and, in a wry understatement, the deep unhappy meditation of anxious human beings), the wind's music to sway to, bowing graciously in the breeze, the evening dew to wear like the rich pearls of a duchess. And even in death, the simple beauty remains, its fragrance comprehended in the fields (like faint-scented spices), its dream-filled sleep in the imposing farms (a striking contrast with the dead in their cold stark graves is perhaps implied). No wonder the poet wishes she were "a hay" (her early editors changed the article to "*the* hay" on the basis of a stricter logic, but the charm of individuality and the simple humanity intrinsic in Miss Dickinson's "*a* hay" gives a keener sense of her intention I believe).

The lyric is written in common meter, following a regular pattern (with the exception of the substitution of a pause for the final accented syllable of line 11, a significant break in the pattern to avoid monotony). The poet's love of alliteration is evident throughout in the phonetic echoes (*g*rass-*g*reen, *s*o-*s*phere-*s*imple-*s*tir-*s*unshine, and *b*utterflies-*b*rood-*b*ees-*b*reezes-*b*ow in stanzas one and two; *d*ews-*d*uchess-*d*ies-*d*ivine-*d*ream-*d*ays-*d*o, *l*ike-*l*owly-*l*ain, and *s*pices-*s*pike-nards-*s*overeign in stanzas three through five).

The syntactic arrangement as a whole is interesting. The opening line raises the expectation of an immediate conclusion, but that expectation is not fulfilled until the final line. All that comes between is a listing of the values upon which the conclusion rests. The lyric thus has the effect of a single periodic sentence, holding us off until the very last word has been said. The rime as well reinforces the effect, its slant delaying satisfaction until the final perfect rime (*away-hay*). (Note the effect of the *fine -ing, -vine -ing* rimes in stanzas three and four; they are, in a sense, perfect, but the mates separated some distance from one another.)

I Know That He Exists (338)

As in many of the lyrics composed in 1862, here is evident the severe emotional crisis which Emily Dickinson was passing through in that year. She was greatly disturbed over Wadsworth's leaving, and she tried to compensate her grief partly by initiating correspondence with Higginson. She began to dress in white at this point as well, as if perpetually ready to wed. Since Wadsworth was a clergyman, her grief often turned upon questions of religion, as it does here.

Her anguish leads to doubt, doubt to despair. The assurance of the opening line is destroyed in the terror that perhaps God does not exist at all. Perhaps the "play," the "jest," the hide-and-seek by which God has kept Himself remote from His creatures is no game at all, but the bleak affirmation that He does not exist. The tone of the lyric's first half, that of the child's acceptance of the situation as an adolescent "play," is reversed starkly as the lyric focusses upon the terror of death when, in its first instant of anticipated confrontation with the enigmatic God, it discovers He never existed at all.

The unusual meter, the short lines in danger of sing-song in the hands of many poets, is masterfully controlled, the startling quality of disorder supported in the want of rime:

```
    //   x/   x/
    /x   x/x
    /x   /x   //
    x/   //

 5  xx/  x/
    xx/  /x
    /x   //
    (x)/ x/   x/

    /x   x/
10  //   x/x
    /x   //
    x/   //

    x/   x/
    //   x/x
    x/   x/
15  x/   //
```

The heavy accents throughout create the essential gravity of the lines. Note particularly the "grossness" of the three clustered accents at the end of line 4, the emphasis given the alliterative "*play* / *P*rove *p*iercing" in stanza three by the three accents. Similarly, "Death's *s*tiff *s*tare" (stanza three) and "crawled too far" (stanza four) struggle under the burden of vocal stress.

The lyric abounds again in musical character, the orchestration of alliteration (*s*omewhere-*s*ilence and *h*e-*h*as-*h*id-*h*is in stanza one; *p*lay-*p*rove-*p*iercing, *g*lee-*g*laze, and *s*tiff-*s*tare in stanza three; *f*un-*f*ar in stanza four), assonance (h*i*d-h*i*s and *I*-s*i*lence-l*i*fe-*eye*s in stanza one; *ea*rn-h*e*r-s*u*rprise in stanza two; pl*a*y-gl*a*ze-st*a*re in stanza three), and consonance (somewhe*r*e-*r*are-ou*r* in stanza one; ea*r*n-he*r*-ow*n*-su*r*prise in stanza two) binding the lines tightly together.

After Great Pain, a Formal Feeling Comes (341)

Emily Dickinson calculates here the creation of a gloomy, funereal, somber tone to convey the stupor which sets in upon her in the experience of psychic anguish. She does not make that creation her only goal, however—we come at last to the final moment—the remarkably precise and poignant simile of death: that sequence of chill, stupor, and letting go experienced by those who have wrestled with the cold of winter and lost.

Of the ten syllables in the first line, six are accented, giving the first half of the line a more particular gravity:

/x   //   x/   x/   x/

The same effect weights and holds back the starts of the second and third lines:

x/   //   x/   xx   x/
x/   //   xx   x/   x/

Momentarily the weight is lifted, but the final line repeats the effect:

//   //   x/   x/   x/

The gloom itself is overridden in the second stanza of the lyric by its bright musical pattern of accent:

x/   x/   xx   //
x/   x/   x/
x/   x/
x/   x/
x/   x/   xx   x/

But the carefree quality (the feet moving without regard for where they are going) must be stopped abruptly or no one will listen to the gravity of the sense very long—and so the trochee at the start of the third stanza slows us down for the somber image of death at the end:

/x   x/   x/

Cleanth Brooks and Robert Penn Warren, in their brilliant analysis of this lyric (*Understanding Poetry,* New York, 1950, pp. 324-327), suggest the progress of words (*formal, ceremonious, stiff, mechanical, wooden, quartz, stone, lead*), each adding a new aspect of thought to the heaviness and stiffening of the psychic experience.

It is clear, of course, that Miss Dickinson had in mind some pain other than a mere physiological suffering. It is in the nature of a psychological or spiritual shock (perhaps even the death of a loved friend), left ambiguous in the interest of an easier identification on the reader's part. Her expression of personal grief becomes the utterance of our own experiences of anguish.

I Dreaded That First Robin So (348)

This is another lyric of the spring of 1862, conveying the poet's mental anguish, comparing her grief to the Passion of Christ (she is "Queen of Calvary"—note too that Christ's Passion is the sacrament of spring, symbol of death and renewal of life). When it was first published in *Poems* (1891), the lyric had been entitled "In Shadow" by its editors. So overcome by grief is the poet that she cannot bear to face the first signs of life and spring in nature. She had hoped they would all be silent in deference to her "passion," but instead, each arrives at its prescribed moment in a radiance of life that makes her depression all the more obvious.

She accepts each harbinger as it greets her, though each "hurts" her with its reckless gaity. The robin's first greeting has come and she has survived it (note the exaggerated metaphor of the "pianos," the host of bird-musicians in the wood). The yellow-gowned daffodil (a personification) has come to hurt her with its radiance. The first signs of grass, the first bees swooping from flower to flower—all are alien to her distempered spirit. Yet they have all come to give their share of hurt to the suffering poet, and she must lift her "childish plumes" to acknowledge their arrival (the drums suggest a parade through the streets, perhaps the implication is that it is a memorial parade honoring the dead, each of the natural signs serving as a "flag" passing in review).

The meter is generally regular, following the pattern of common measure. There are implied pauses at the ends of lines 11 and 13, but few other irregularities (note the strong effect of the spondaic foot at the beginning of line 7, breaking the pattern slightly to call attention to its significance). The lyric is not so marked by alliteration as are many of the others (note, however, *h*im-*h*e-*h*urts in stanza one; *p*ianos-*p*ower in stanza two; *d*ared-*d*affodils in stanza three; *t*oo-*t*all-*t*allest in stanza four; *b*ear-*b*ees in stanza five; *q*ueen-*C*alvary in stanza six), the tone being generally more stayed, more sober and depressing than usual.

I Felt My Life with Both My Hands (351)

The poet has experienced a trial so devastating that it has left her unsure of her own person, unable to be positive that she is indeed the person she was. She examines this new creature to assure herself that it is she, holding her very being up to view (as one would examine himself in a mirror—a glass) to prove the reality of it (to see if it is "possible" that it is real and the same). She inquires the "name" of this "being" to see if it were familiar to her. She probes and tests every detail of her person to gain the "conviction" that this is herself, engaging finally in a dialog with herself (her "friend"), encouraging herself that she may come to like this new being as well as she had the old.

The lyric is in common meter, though the arrangement obscures that fact in stanzas two and three. In stanza two, the first two syllables of the last line should stand at the end of the previous line; in stanza three, the last three syllables of the second line should stand at the start of the third. (Such misplacing of metric feet is common in Miss Dickinson's manuscripts. So intent was she upon the meanings of the lines that she often did not place them quite accurately on the page.)

Again the phonetic echoes are a strong part of the success. Note the reversal of consonants in *felt-life* (line 1), as well as the frequent alliteration: *prove-possible-paused-pound* (stanzas one and two), *judged-jarred* (line 9), *told-take* (line 13), *friend-former* (lines 13-14), *learn-like* (line 15), *heaven-home* (lines 15-16).

God Is a Distant, Stately Lover (357)

Emily Dickinson puts a fundamental theological assertion into a childlike allegory, fitting her doctrine to the legendary account of Miles Standish's vicarious courtship of Priscilla for John Alden. The charm of her unconventionality understates the deeper religious meaning, robbing it of its profundity. When it was first printed in *The Christian Register* (April 2, 1891), the simple lyric outraged a number of readers who felt it contemptuous, failing to comprehend its tone of naive reverence.

The lyric reminds us of #338, "I know that He exists," both written in the same year. The earlier lyric, however, grapples with the terrors of doubt, while this focusses upon the identity of God as revealed in the two persons of Father and Son. At the start, Emily

Dickinson alludes to such Biblical passages as John III:16 ("For God so loved the world that He gave His only begotten Son") and to Hebrews I:1-2 ("God, who at sundry times and in divers manners spake in time past unto the fathers by the prophets, hath in these last days spoken unto us by His Son").

The vocabulary may be deliberately "learned," an effort to seem intellectual, while the analogy denies such an effect. "Vicarious," for example, is the traditional theological term for the atonement, one dying in the stead of another. The "hyperbolic archness" partly obscures the meaning ("exaggerated mischief"), continuing the playful contradiction within the lyric. The high degree of compression produces a number of awkward syntactic moments (for example, "as He states us" and "synonym" for synonymous).

The meter is highly irregular, shifting in stress erratically, but supporting generally the emphases intended:

```
  /xx /x  /x  /x    (or)    /x  x/  x/  x/x
  /x  x/  x/  x/
  /x  /xx /xx /x
  /x  x/  xx/ x/
5 /xx /x  /x  /x    (or)    /x  x/  x/  x/x
  /x  /x  x/  x/
  /xx /x  /x  /x
  /x  //  xx/ x/
```

Each line opens with a stress which supports the importance of the words at the starts of the lines (even "But" has a significant weight in the meaning as the hinge upon which the contrast between Miles and Priscilla—God and Christ—turns). The feet are predominantly dactyllic and trochaic, though Emily Dickinson prefers the finality of the iamb at the ends of the second and fourth lines of each stanza.

The rimes are, in the first stanza, perfect (*Son-one*), but in the second dissonant (*Groom-synonym*). There are numerous instances of alliteration (*stately-states-Son-soul-spurn-synonym; verily-vicarious-vouches*), assonance (*verily-vicarious*), and consonance (*distant-stately-states-us, vicarious-courtship, Priscilla-such-lest-soul-Priscilla-like, vouches-archness*).

Death Sets a Thing Significant (360)

First published in *Poems* (1891) under the title "Memorials," the lyric commemorates the deaths of the poet's friends and contains a particular allusion to Ben Newton (who had given her "a book" before his death, a well-marked copy of Emerson's *Poems*). The young lawyer's apprentice had been the poet's "teacher," but had died in 1853. The subject is the manner in which death "italicizes" simple events, making them seem significant in a way they had not otherwise been. The dead entreat us through simple objects.

There are the little drawing which is all the more important when the child who wrought it dies soon after, the needlework left unfinished by the death of its craftsman, and, most significantly, the book held once in the hands of the dead youth whose pencillings in the margin bring tears to the poet's eyes. The closing line is puzzling and ambiguous, suggesting perhaps that the etchings, now "obliterated" by the poet's tears (not simply that she cannot see them, but that her tears have stained and ruined the pages containing them), cannot be replaced because they are part of a book made valuable by "his" having held and marked it; such a book could never be restored, since he is dead.

The lyric is composed in common meter, but with pauses required at the ends of lines 3, 9, 13, 15, 17, and 19. The required hesitations (in each case to fill out the expectations of the iambic pentameter line) give a quality of meditation to the whole. The rimes are imperfect (except in stanza three), providing the slight dissonance which the subject requires.

Again the musical effects abound, alliteration (*h*ad-*h*urried in line 2; *w*orkmanships-*w*ool-*w*ith-*w*as-*w*eighed in lines 5-9; *st*itches-*st*opped in line 10; *p*encil-*p*lace-*pl*eased in lines 14-15; *t*ears-*t*oo in lines 18, 20), assonance (d*ea*th-s*e*ts in line 1; *eye*-b*ye*, internal rime, in line 2; *e*xcept-*e*ntreat-t*e*nderly in lines 3-4; *i*n-*i*n-w*i*th-th*i*s-f*i*ngers-d*i*d-*i*ndustrious-unt*i*l-th*i*mble-st*i*tches in lines 6-10), and consonance (dea*th*-*th*ing in line 1; ha*d*-hurrie*d*-perishe*d* in lines 2-3; excep*t*-*t*en*tr*ea*t*-*t*enderly-*t*o-li*tt*le in lines 3-5; thi*s*-la*s*t-indu*s*triou*s* in lines 7-8; hav*e*-gav*e* in line 13; he*re*-the*re* in line 14; in*t*errup*t*ing-*t*ears-obli*t*era*t*e-*t*oocos*t*ly, fo*r*-*r*epairs in lines 19-20) heard echoing throughout.

Dare You See a Soul at the White Heat? (365)

Entitled "The White Heat" both in its first publication in *Atlantic Monthly* (October 1891) and in *Poems* (1891), the lyric was published a number of times as four four-line stanzas, rather than as a sixteen-line unit. Again we see reflected the anguished state of spirit so characteristic of the lyrics of 1862.

The basic metaphor of the blacksmith at the forge, hammering out his metalwork, represents the soul at the mercy of the eternal Blacksmith (God), who hammers and shapes her being to suit His own ends. She alludes to the symbol consistently; it is one frequently used by the clergy to show the necessity of suffering as a fulfillment of God's purpose in shaping human souls after His will. The bulk of the lyric focusses upon the literal blacksmith at his forge, but the meaning centers in our comprehension of its basic metaphorical sense.

Divided into quatrains as suggested above, the lyric is in common measure, stressed syllables omitted at the ends of lines 5 and 9 (the stresses to be taken in pause). Only the first line is complicatedly irregular: /x /x /xx //. It appears to avoid the iambic of the rest of the poem altogether. Perhaps its unusual meter is meant to single out the abstract statement, to fix it within the mind before the metaphor of the forge takes the foreground. The rime (while the first quatrain is a repetition of sounds: *door* — vivi*d ore*) is imperfect, *blaze* and *forge* serving in both the second and fourth quatrains. Alliteration (*see-soul* in line 1, *dare-door* in lines 1 and 2, *vivid-vanquished* in lines 4-5, *flame's-forge* in lines 5-6, *light-least* in lines 7 and 9, *blaze-blacksmith* in lines 8-9, *stands-symbol-soundless* and *for-finer-forge* in lines 11-12) and consonance (*white-heat* in line 1, *red-is-fire's* and *within-common-tint-when-vanquished-conditions* in lines 2-5, *vivid-vanquished-quivers-village-anvil* in lines 4-6, 9-10) are basic poetic devices by which the lyric is developed.

She Lay as If at Play (369)

Here, as in a number of her lyrics, Emily Dickinson looks straight at death, at the still corpse, seeking to describe its appearance. The practice strikes us as morbid at first, but in reality the poet achieves such imaginative effects that the morbidity is not disturbing. In this portrait she carries out the motif of play in the child's death. For an instant the child has been caught in the motionlessness of death, like a motion picture suddenly stopped.

As the child leaps, life leaps from her (yet with the intention to return—in resurrection?), causing a moment's lull in her play (a lull from which she cannot return to action). Even her eyes are "sparkling" in youthful fun behind the half-closed lids, as though only pretending as such a child might when her mother cracks the door to see if she is still asleep.

The metric pattern is oddly laid out, the first two quatrains containing three iambic trimeter lines with a fourth iambic dimeter, and the latter two containing two iambic trimeter lines followed by two iambic dimeter lines. The effect is itself a "trick" such as one might associate with the child, the teasing shorter lines falling short of our expectation. These brief lines too help to create the sense of the child's world, having the catch-like rhythm of the nursery rime. The rime scheme as well (unusual for Emily Dickinson—aabb) brings the sound echoes within such proximity as to create a "jingly" quality, one which might destroy the gravity of the subject altogether were it not tempered by the imperfection of the rimes (*-turn-soon, dropt-sport, -got-start, jar-were, door-sure*). The internal rime at the start (*lay-play-away*) initiates the playful spirit, but that tone is quickly subdued in the imperfect rimes which follow (the effect is repeated in the last stanza: *morning-door*).

The concentrated alliterations of the lyric (*lay-life-leaped* in lines 1 and 2, *so-soon* in line 4, *sport-start* in lines 6 and 8, *still-sparkling* in line 11, *for-fun-force* in lines 12 and 15, *door-devising-deep* in lines 13-15, 16) undergird the fanciful quality of the utterance, themselves a part of the poetic game. Consonance (note, for example, he*r-merry-arm*s-d*r*opt-fo*r*-*sport*-fo*r*got-t*r*ick-*start* in stanza two) and assonance (for example, de*v*ising-*I*-*l*ight in stanza four) contribute further to the sense of delight.

I'm Saying Every Day (373)

First published in *Atlantic Monthly* (November 1935) with the title "If I Should Be a Queen," the lyric expresses the poet's child-like imaginative projection of herself into some royal role. She raises the speculation: "Suppose I were a noble woman tomorrow—would I be prepared for such an adventure?" It is the dream of the rustic, the romantic hope of social advancement. First it is as queen she imagines herself, wondering how she would dress for so awesome a position. Perhaps she will be a member of the royal Bourbon family, that politically and socially reactionary clan that ruled France and Spain and parts of Italy at times in the sixteenth through the nineteenth centuries; if she does awaken in such a revered role, she does not wish to be recognized as the girl who begged the day before in the marketplace.

Wrapping her apron about her, looping it with buttercups, she

dreams of standing in the ranks of nobility. She strives for the grand
language of court, though her only subjects may be the cricket and
the bee. Nonetheless, she will be prepared lest she should find herself
in Aragon or summoned to Exeter, dressed only in the primitive garb
of her rustic life.

The meter and stanziac pattern (as well as the rime) of the lyric
are highly irregular:

```
    //   x/   x/                  a
    x/   x/   x/   x/x            b
    x/   //                       a
    x/   x/   x/x                 c

 5  /x   /x   /x   /x             a
    /x   //   /x   /xx            b
    x/   x/                       c
    /x   x/   x/                  b
    /x   /(x)?                    c

10  /x   x/   x/                  a    (note c in the previous stanza)
    x/   //                       b
    /x   /x   /xx   /x   /xx      b
    x/   /x   /x   /(x)           c
    x/   //                       d
15  /xx   /x                      b

    x/   x/                       a
    x/   x/   x/   x/             b
    x/   x/x   //                 c
    x/   x/                       b

20  /xx   /x   //   //            a
    x/   x/x   x/   x/            a
    x/   xx/   x/                 b
    x/   xx/                      c
    /x   /x   /x                  d
25  /x   //                       c

    /x   /x   /x                  a
    x/   //                       b
    /xx   /xx                     b
    x/   //                       b
```

```
30   xx   x/   /(x)                a
     /x   /(x)                     a
     (x)/   x/   x/   x/           b
     x/   x/                       a
```

(Note that, in analyzing the rime, I have begun again in each stanza, though the form is so irregular that to make the assumption that there are stanzas is questionable. The lyric was left rough by the poet, and, while it has a charm in its childlike fantasy, it is not in finished form. It is the nearest Miss Dickinson ever came to practicing free verse— she had heard of Whitman, but hesitated to read his verse because of the scandal associated with it.)

Here is well illustrated Miss Dickinson's accustomed reliance upon alliteration (*be-Bourbon-bend-begged* in stanza two, *tongue-twigs-term* in stanza four, *meadow-morn-meet-me-my* in stanzas five and six), assonance (*saying-day* in line 1, *be-queen* in line 2, *stately-place-say-plain-overtake* in stanza two, *better-ready-next* in stanza six), and consonance (*stately-place-say-so-loop-apron-pins-plain* in stanza three, *than-morn-Aragon-gown-on* in stanza six, *surprised-air-rustics-wear-Exeter* in stanza seven).

Of Course I Prayed (376)

Emily Dickinson bespeaks her spiritual anguish, turning her despair toward God and His failure to hear her prayer. The opening air of assurance (*of course*) is swept away in the questioning of God's concern. The absurd image of the poet as a bird stomping its foot ridiculously on the air as if demanding what it is useless to demand, is ironically contrasted with the gravity of her situation, a matter of life and death (she would die unless he lives). She had rather never to have been born, to have enjoyed the senselessness of a consciousless (dead) atom, than to bear the "smart" of her present trial (note the noun *smart*'s use as an adjective here).

The bewilderment of mind is admirably caught in the awkwardness of the metric form (though some of the difficulty is resolved if lines were rearranged: line 3 is actually two dimeter lines, as are lines 9 and 10. Thus the stanzaic pattern is the quintain, with four dimeter lines and a fifth iambic trimeter line).

1	x/ x/		a	prayed
2	x/ //		b	care
3 {	x/ x/		c	much
	x/ x/		b	air
4	x/ x/ x/		d	foot
5	x/ //		a	me
6	x/ x/		b	life
7 {	x/ x/		c	had
	x/ x/		b	-self
8	x/ x/ x/		a	-ty
9 {	x/ x/		a	in
	x/ x/		b	tomb
10 {	/x x/		c	nought
	x/ x/		b	dumb
11	x/ // x/		d	-ry

While *care* and *air* of stanza one (in the suggested rearrangement of the lines) are perfect rimes, *life-self* (stanza two) and *tomb-dumb* (stanza three) are appropriately slant. *Foot* (stanza one) dangles without a rime, but *charity* (stanza two) and *misery* (stanza three) echo each other clearly, setting up a poignant contrast of meanings.

The metric substitutions create significant effects, the trochaic foot at the start of line 10, followed by the lilt of the monosyllables, creates a moment of gaity before the slow spondee of the last line. In the second line, the placing of the word *God* in a syllable not ordinarily accented, gives it particular emphasis through surprise (the same is true of *give* in line 5, where the absurdity of the demand is stressed).

Exhilaration Is Within (383)

Emily Dickinson strives to convey the abstract state of exhilaration by the concrete image of intoxication (the "outer" wine). All the time she is developing the comparison, she insists upon the superiority of the soul's stimulation. Added to the image of intoxication is that of religious ecstasy (the wine of the sacrament serving to yoke together the two). The man whose "closet" is amply stocked with the best wines (the spiritual means of exhilaration) cannot be excited very fully by the merely external stimuli. Exhilaration lies within her soul.

The meter is an odd mixture, stanza one composed in common measure, stanzas two and three in short measure. The slant rime of the first (*wine-brand*) and last (*Rhine-offering*) stanzas sustains again the sense of intoxication. The echoes of alliteration in *soul-set-sacrament-stimulate* illustrate her fondness for sibilance.

No Rack Can Torture Me (384)

Entitled "Emancipation" by its editors when it first appeared in *Poems* (1890), the lyric starts by declaring the Senecan dogma of the soul's utter freedom from all enslavement, but ends by admitting that the soul can enslave itself if at odds with itself (thus paradoxically consciousness can be both the essence of liberty and of bondage). Of particular interest is the metaphorical development of the soul as another "body." Its "bone" is bolder than the flesh's, unable to be broken by the torturer's rack or saw. Adding to that fundamental metaphor a second comparison (that of the eagle), the poet generates the image of the birdlike soul fleeing triumphantly from its nestlike body. Yet the final caution of the torment of internal strife, if inescapable, suggests the poet's trials of this period.

The stanzaic pattern starts out regularly (the iambic trimeter quatrain), full of confidence and steady assertion. But it jogs somewhat awkwardly in its last two stanzas, the third shortening its two final lines, the fourth containing dimeter, trimeter, and tetrameter lines:

```
III   x/   x/   x/
      x/   x/   x/
      x/   x/
      x/   x/

IV    x/   x/   x/
      //   x/
      x/   x/   x/   x/
      //   x/
```

The same may be said generally of the rime. The stanzas begin with the scheme aabb (though *bone-one* and *be-fly* are clearly slant; *scimitar* and *saw* may be nearer in the New England dialect than at first appears). However, in stanza three, *sky* saves itself for the eye-rime of *enemy* and *liberty, consciousness* having no mate (unless *nest* is meant to satisfy our expectation). At any rate, the point is clear that what begins as a confident lyric ends somewhat shakily in the nervous agitation of the latter two stanzas. The effect appears deliberate, reinforcing the sense of the whole.

The entire lyric abounds in echoes of sound: *rack-ca*n, *behind-bon*e-*bold*er-*bod*ies-*b*e-*b*ind, *s*aw-*sc*imitar, *nest-n*o, *ea*gle-*ea*sier, *than-th*ou-*th*yself-*th*ine, *ex*cept-*en*emy, *ca*ptivity-*co*n*sc*iou*sne*ss, etc., showing the poet's care for phonetic repetitions.

There's Been a Death in the Opposite House (389)

Emily Dickinson, with deft brush, sketches the telling details of a nineteenth-century death. The house itself is shrouded in numbness. The neighbors come and go. The physician leaves; the death mattress is thrown out to be destroyed (a custom still observed in some regions), the curious children speculating whether the corpse died upon this mattress (the poet envisions herself a boy sharing their curiosity). The pastor takes possession of the house and the grieving relatives (his mastery extends even to the "little boys," usually not so attentive to him). The stark figures of the funeral arrive: the milliner to fashion a fitting attire for burial, the mortician to construct a casket of proper dimension. All is in readiness for the solemn and ceremonial procession to the cemetery. The poet's mind knows intuitively that death has come to her small village.

The meter of the lyric, while basically common measure, contains numerous substitutions. In the first stanza, for example, the third line contains only three stresses and creates an effect of shortness (balanced off by the slow stretch of the first line):

```
      x/   x/   xx/  xx/
      x/   x/   x/
      x/x  xx   //
      //   x/   x/

  5   x/   x/   x/   x/
      x/   x/   x/
      x/   x/   x/   x/
      x/   x/   (x)x/

      /x   x/   x/   x/
```

```
10   x/   x/   x/
     x/   x/   x/   x/
     //   x/   x/

     x/   xx   //   x/
     x/   x/   x/
15   x/   //   x/   x/
     x/   x/   x/

     x/   x/   xx   xx/
     xx   x/   x/
     x/   x/   xx   x/
20   x/   x/   x/

     x/   xx   x/   x/
     x/   x/   x/
     x/   x/   xx   x/
     x/   x/   x/
```

The steady, uninterrupted beat of the second stanza comes to abrupt pause in the opening trochee of the third stanza, and the tempo is slowed again by the spondees of lines 12 and 15. The caesuras (pauses) of lines 8 and 17 lend time as well for the assimilation of meaning. All in all, the alternation of rapid and slow pace is skillfully managed.

This lyric, like so many others, makes use of alliteration (*know*-*numb*-*neighbors* in stanzas one and two, *houses*-*have* in stanza one, *doctor*-*drives* in stanza two, *mechanically*-*mattress*-*minister*-*mourners*-*milliner*-*man*-*measure* in stanzas two through five, *by*-*boy*-*boys*-*besides* in stanzas three and four, *trade*-*take*-*tassels*-*town* in stanzas five and six), assonance (*lately*-*today* in stanza one, *window*-*opens* in stanza two, *minister*-*stiffly*-*in*-*if*-*his* in stanza four), and consonance (*somebody*-*children*-*wonder*-*died*-*used* in stanza three, *owned*-*mourners*-*now* in stanza four, *stiffly*-*all*-*little*-*milliner*-*appalling* in stanzas four and five).

The special cacophony of sibilants is also exploited (*there's*-*opposite*-*house*-*as*-*as*-*such*-*houses*-*neighbors*-*rustle*-*drives*-etc.). There is here a curious effect at the ends of the first lines of stanzas two through four: "in and out" is echoed first in the "out" of stanza three and then in the "in" of stanza four, focussing the reader's mind upon the continual motion to and from the house, the clue to the intuition that there has been a death in the neighboring house.

What Soft Cherubic Creatures (401)

Scorn is rare in the Emily Dickinson lyric, but here it is given full reign as the poet looks sarcastically at the "gentlewomen" of her world. So "gentle" are they, so "soft" (like the "plush" of velvet), so angelic (cherublike), one dares not affront them with the vulgarity of common humanity. Their convictions are dimity (the fine cotton thread used in expensive garments), their sense of what is shocking (horror) so refined that it is not only appalled by the flaws of human nature, but ironically embarrassed by the "crudeness" of God Himself, especially His lack of sensitivity in having given the lowly fisherman Peter the keys to the kingdom. Thus the untutored, rough seaman is given the privilege of bestowing the degree redemption, a circumstance appalling to the "gentlewomen" of Emily Dickinson's day.

The meter of the lyric, the common measure of the New England hymnal, is steady and predictable, except that every odd line except the third contains an elision of the final accented syllable. Such elisions are usually satisfied in pause, a retardation of the line endings apparently arranged to allow more careful assimilation of meaning.

The rimes of the first and third stanzas are perfect, though that of the second is only consonantal (*refined-ashamed*). There are instances here of the piling up of consonant clusters to create a slower, more selfconscious effect in oral recitation (e. g., *What soft cherubic creatures / These gentlewomen* are. . . . *Such dimity convictions / A horror so refined / Of freckled human nature*, etc.). The sibilants of the opening stanza create just the right cacophony to lead us to doubt the assertions of impeccable breeding.

They Dropped Like Flakes (409)

Entitled by its original editors (*Poems,* 1891) "The Battle-Field" and composed early in the days of the Civil War, the lyric suggests its origins in some new devastation of the conflict. Its thesis is the seeming indifference of nature to the deaths afield as contrasted with God's infinite concern and recollection at each falling. It suggests the Biblical assertion that not a sparrow falls but that God notes and records it.

The chief effect of the lyric is to suggest in a sequence of similes what it is like for the men to die—like snow that falls, melts, and is forgotten, like stars that streak across the skies and burn themselves out, like the petals of a rose that flutter from the stem without notice, blown by the winds of June. They have fallen in the grass which contains no imprint of their bodies, no marker of their having fallen. Their lot is oblivion, except that God keeps in His mind the memory of each face and notes each in His list (presumably the Book of Life which contains the names of the redeemed; see Revelation XX:12-15).

The stanzaic pattern is that of common measure (though the first line is actually here divided into two: x/ x/ — x/ x/). The rime of the first stanza is perfect (*rose-goes*), but the second is odd in that the expected placement of rime (*place-list*) is imperfect, while lines 2 and 3 (*place-face*) are rimed perfectly. The entire last stanza's rime seems composed of a consonantal echo of the *s* sound (*grass-place-face-list*).

The repetitive sound echoes create a music which intensifies the lyric's beauty (e. g., *like-flak*es, *wind-with-finger*s-*goes*, *seamless-grass*, *repeal*less-*list*). The syntactic organization is interesting:

> They dropped like flakes . . . .
> They dropped like stars . . . .
> 　　　　　like petals . . . .
> They perished . . . .
> No one could find . . . .
> But God can summon . . . .

The syntactic repetitions bind the lyric together tightly.

The First Day's Night Had Come (410)

Written in 1862, that year noted in the Dickinson biography both for its emotional turmoil and its enormous output of poetry, this lyric describes the poet's endurance of great psychic trial and the effect of the crisis upon her mind. She dramatizes the incident as though she and her soul were separate beings communicating with one another. One day had ended—she had endured the trial of that "first day"; she had wanted her soul to sing, but her soul (now metaphorically the violin or other stringed instrument itself) too requires mending (a task keeping her from the rest she needs).

As the new day dawns, the severity of trial is twice that of yesterday. So horrifying is this new terror that the mind snaps; broken by the strain, it laughs in compensating madness. As the years have passed, the derangement has never been set right; the madness continues until this moment.

The lyric is composed in a regular short-meter pattern, the rime of the first stanza the only perfect one. The dissonance of *blown-morn, pairs-eyes, fool-still,* and *was-this* providing the appropriate bewilderment to the whole. The spondee of the first line (x/ // x/), added to the consonant clusterings (*the first day's night had come*), gives a slow melancholy weight to the start. The predominance of sibilant sounds points to the cacophony of the whole (e. g., *soul-sing-she-said-strings-snapt; keeps-still-something's-person-was-this-same-madness-this*).

The Color of the Grave Is Green (411)

Emily Dickinson describes the grave as it appears from without to us the living (first in summer, then in winter) and then suggests that there is an inner "grave" too, much different from this outer one. At first we imagine she is describing the interior of an actual grave, but it becomes at once obvious she means that part of the "grave" we carry within us, the continued grief which lies within the soul of the bereaved.

In summer, the "outer" grave, the exterior of the actual burial spot, is green, undifferentiated from the rest of the landscape except by the grave marker erected to guide the "fond" to the spot where the body lies (with a childlike naïveté, the poet points to the sleeping corpse which cannot speak up to direct the mourner; hence the need for the stone marker). In winter, one could not find the grave often for the high drifts which obscure both grave and marker; but when the sun has melted the snow, then we can see the grave in relief, a mound standing slightly above the rest of the terrain which has sunken lower than the soil above the casket.

But there is a "duplicate" grave within the mourner. It cannot be affected by the snows of winter or the sun of summer. It is a grief (a "grave") stirred by the sight which recalls to the mind the departed dead, though it lies so deeply within that no ferret (a weasel which burrows in the earth) can arrive at it.

The stanzaic pattern is again the common measure of the hymnal, accented syllables omitted at the ends of lines 5, 13, and 21. The rimes are generally and appropriately dissonant (*mean-stone, mean-*

sun, land-friend, bound-find), though in stanzas two and five they are perfect. As so often elsewhere, we find here her frequent use of alliteration (*grave-green-grave, not-kn*ow in stanza one; *from-field-fond-find* in stanzas one and two; *daisy-deep* in stanza two; *bonnet-bound-before* and *ferret-find* in stanza six), assonance (*own-stone* in stanza one; th*an*-l*and* and l*eft*-fr*iend* in stanza four, gr*een*-s*een* in stanzas five and six) and consonance (f*ond*-fi*nd,* h*elp*-a*sleep*-*stop*-dee*p* in stanza two).

I Read My Sentence Steadily (412)

Undoubtedly related again to the emotional crisis of 1862, the lyric dramatizes the poet's sense of condemnation in her present condition. Doomed to martyrdom, she is death's friend, and the terror of the grave cannot frighten her. In the drama, she is a condemned criminal who reads her sentence without wincing. There are no heroics, but no sentimentality either: only a simple acceptance of her fate (note again the division of soul and poet in the enactment of the drama). The soul, knowing her fate, apparently enacts the execution again and again, so that, when the final moment comes, it is no novel experience for her.

When it first appeared in *Poems* (1891), the lyric was arranged as four common measure stanzas, lines 9 and 10 actually containing two lines each:

```
       x/   x/   x/   x/
       x/   x/   x/
       x/   x/   //   x/
       x/   x/   x/

   5   x/   x/   x/   x/
       x/   x/   x/
       x/   //   x/   x/
       x/   x/   x/

   9  {x/   x/   x/   x(/)
      {x/   x/   x/
  10  {x/   x/   x/   x/
      {x/   x/   x/

       x/   x/   x/   x(/)
       //   x/   x/
```

$$x/ \quad x/ \quad x/ \quad x/$$
$$x/ \quad x/ \quad x/$$

The rime, while consistently slant (*eyes-clause, form-him, extremity-agony*) except for the last stanza (*friends-ends*), bears out the four-stanza arrangement.

I Never Felt at Home Below (413)

The paradox of the soul, feeling uncomfortable under the continual surveillance of God on earth and in the promise of His eternal presence with her in heaven, half wanting to flee from God and yet terrified by the alternatives: that is the theme of this lyric. Always unorthodox in her attitude toward the "Sabbath" and conventional notions of Christianity, Emily Dickinson nonetheless carried with her throughout life a consciousness of God (and often a fear of Him, though at times she is notably flippant). She rejects the traditional Christian "idea" as dreadfully dull, and yet she fears God's wrath against those who despise Him.

She does not long for an eternal Sunday, a perpetual Eden where there is no relief from the bliss. If only God would go off on a visit, such that He could not see us, the poet would run off, escape Him altogether. But she is frustrated by her conviction of judgment, knowing that nothing escapes the vigilant eye of God which has us under constant survey.

The lyric is composed in common measure, a somewhat ironic meter here, since her message contradicts that of the traditional "hymn" for which the stanzaic pattern served (note that accented syllables are omitted at the ends of lines 7, 9, and 13). The rimes are again largely slant (*skies-paradise, comes-afternoons, nap-telescope*), conveying her dissatisfaction with the state of things.

Much Madness Is Divinest Sense (435)

The lyric is built on the paradox that often what appears reasonable to one man may seem idiotic to another. Unfortunately, the "majority" rule. It may well be in some cases that the majority is itself mad, the individual's "madness" a most sensible alternative. Yet, if the individual will not give way to the majority's will, he is considered "dangerous" and placed under lock and key. With gentle irony, the lyric argues for the individual and against the concept of the natural and inevitable superiority of the mass. It has been called Emersonian in doctrine because of its appeal to individual self-reliance (one of the volumes Ben Newton had given Emily Dickinson was a well-marked collection of Emerson's poems).

Editors often arrange the lines as two quatrains, the first in common measure (except that the accented syllable of line 3 is elided, requiring an effective pause at that point), the second in short measure. The stanzaic differentiation, however, is unimportant, since the two quatrains run together semantically and syntactically.

The alliteration of *m* (*m*uch-*m*adness-*m*ajority), *d* (*d*ivinest-*d*iscerning-*d*emur-*d*angerous), and *s* (*s*ense-*s*tarkest-*s*ane-*s*traightway) sounds, supported by the frequent sibilant echoes throughout, shows Emily Dickinson's care for the phonetic intricasies of her craft. The clusters of consonant sounds (*Much madness is divinest sense* . . . . *Much sense the starkest madness*) require a slowing of the lines, an effect necessary if the paradox is to be comprehended fully.

Prayer Is the Little Implement (437)

Entitled "Prayer" by its first editors (*Poems,* 1891), the lyric is an effort to "define" prayer in metaphor. Prayer is the tangible means (the "implement") by which men touch heaven, that region to which presence is now denied them. It is like the telegraph (or some such instrument) through which a message can be carried across great voids of space; thus man "flings" his words to God. The sixth line ("If then He hear") conveys a touch of doubt, a mild cynicism perhaps substantiated by the odd word "fling" and by the whole effort to reduce the spiritual act to concrete image (the reduction of prayer to an "apparatus").

The gently mocking tone is caught too in the awkward metric, the alternation of tetrameter and dimeter lines, with elision and awkward substitution:

```
  /x  x/  x/  x/
  x/  //
  x/  xx  x/  x(/)
  x/  //
5 x/  x/  x/  /(?)
  x/  //
```

```
        //  x/  x/  x(/)
        x/  x/
```

The "cute" echoes of the shorter lines (*which-reach, He-hear, comprised-prayer*) detract as well from the seriousness of the subject, the last two lines characterized by laconic irony.

This Is My Letter to the World (441)

Emily Dickinson identifies herself as a "nature" poet. She records in her poems (her "letter") the simple message of the natural landscape, a landscape nonetheless filled with a certain majestic quality. While she has no point of contact with the world of men, no tangible way of knowing their response to her work, she asks her "countrymen" to see in her the same tenderness which she sees in nature, to judge her by her representation of nature.

The stanza form is that of common measure (except that the fifth line has lost its final accented syllable), built on a single rime (*me-majesty-see-me*) which comes full circle to repeat the first person pronoun. Again Miss Dickinson's interest in the effects of sound is clear. Note her use particularly of alliteration (*world-wrote, news-nature, told-tender, majesty-message, committed-cannot-countrymen, simple-see-sweet*).

This Was a Poet—It Is That (448)

It was inevitable that Emily Dickinson should praise the poet's gift, that sensitivity which she herself possessed so fully. The poet (like Wordsworth) can take ordinary objects or events and invest them with amazing and mysterious delight (as one makes exotic perfumes from the lowly blossom which dies at his door). When he gives us his vision, we are always startled by the obviousness of it and wonder how we had missed it. His work is the concretizing of the abstract, the giving of "local habitation" to "airy nothing."

To compare ourselves with him is to become all too conscious of our own "poverty": he is wealthy in his artistic gift (his ability to see and to comprehend with his superb sensitivity); he is his own "fortune," his transcendent talent lifting him above the temporal world.

Written in common measure, the lyric contains few deviations from the pattern (the most notable being the elisions of accented syllables from lines 3, 5, 9, 11, 13, and 15). The opening trochee throws the emphasis to *poet* and also stresses the semantic contrast *this-that*. The strong alliterative effects of the last two stanzas (*p*ictures-*p*oet-*p*overty-*p*ortion, *h*arm-*h*imself-*h*im) combine with the dominance of nasal sounds in the last stanza to enrich the phonetic texture of the passage (which, incidentally, becomes increasingly complex and elliptical).

I Died for Beauty (449)

When Higginson included this lyric with thirteen others in *Christian Union* (September 1890), he gave it the title "Two Kinsmen." There is the obvious debt to Keats' "Ode on a Grecian Urn," in which beauty and truth are viewed as one and the same. The poet had given her life in behalf of beauty. She finds her grave adjoining that of a man who had died for truth. This kinship of "failures" (causes of dying) sets them on a dialogue that, if we may believe the hyperbole, lasts for centuries (much like the philosophers and aestheticians who have debated the questions since ancient times).

The stanza form is common measure, exceptional only in the heavy accents at the start of the first line (//   x/   xx   x/) and the slant rimes of stanzas two (*replied-said*) and three (*rooms-names*). There are numerous interesting phonetic effects (note the nasals of lines 3 and 4, the *f* sounds of lines 5-6, the *-men-met* of line 9, the *t* sounds of lines 9-10). (N. B. *Themself* in line 7 is an "incorrect" syntactic form for *themselves* or, more accurately, *they;* however, note how effectively it catches the ambiguous two and one meaning in its plural-singular fault.)

Love, Thou Art High (453)

The entire lyric is an apostrophe to love, confronting him with the frustration of his unattainability. He is too high to be reached (as high as Chimborazo, the Ecuadorian volcanic mountain), too deep (profound) an ocean to be crossed, too fully veiled for many to see. Yet, were there two in love, perhaps none of the obstacles would be too great for them to conquer. They could take turns climbing until they stand at the mountain's peak; they could tackle any sea and arrive at last even at the sun (as older legends sometimes speak of a ship's sailing into the sun as it sets on the horizon).

The final stanza is less straightforward, more cryptic than the first two. Apparently Miss Dickinson means to suggest the fates of those who do catch a vision of love: they smile, change (perhaps *alter* is meant also to suggest *altar*), prattle (behaving like children), and die. This strange and succinct account of the lover's progress is yet meant to contain its "bliss," that odd state in which lovers find themselves. Much like the bliss of heaven (eternity), love is a spiritual state of being ("God is love"). Love is the recurring symbol of the celestial.

While the lyric is arranged as three six-line stanzas, the rime suggests it is actually in long measure. A simple combination of lines shows that:

1-2	/x	x/	x/	x/x	
3-4	/x	x/	//	x/	we
5	/x	/x	x/	x/x	
6	/x	x/	x/	x/	thee
7-8	/x	x/	x/	x/x	
9-10	/x	x/	x/	x/	one
11	/x	x/	x/	x/x	
12	//	xx	/x	/(?)	sun
13-14	/x	x/	x/	x/x	
15	/x	/x	x/	xx/	die
16	/x	x/	xx	x/x	
17-18	//	x/	x/	x/	eternity

Triumph May Be of Several Kinds (455)

Entitled "Triumph" by its earliest editors (*Poems,* 1891), the lyric classifies the varieties of triumph in human life: (1) the triumph of faith over the imperiousness of death, (2) the triumph of truth over the assaults of falsehood, (3) the triumph of honor over the trial of the bribe, (4) the triumph of a man vindicated at God's final judgment bar. In each of the stanzas, the assertion is dramatized. In the first, it is the wrestling of faith with the powerful enemy death. In the second, truth marches unsullied on with God alone, her supreme Lord (?), standing by to applaude. In the third, the victor hands back temptation's bribe (the promise of some "heaven" of bliss) and faces the torture of the rack. And in the last, the naked just man walks from God's judgment acquitted. Thus the abstract assertions are made concrete.

On the surface the poet appears self-confident. But her casting of four verbs (*be overcome, advance, be handed, pass*) in the subjunctive mode tends to raise some doubt. Is she suggesting, for example: "There is triumph in the room when death is overcome by faith, if indeed death can be overcome by faith at all"? Is it possible she is implying, for example, that the self-assurance of the Calvinists she had heard had not convinced her altogether that eternal life was so certain as they had maintained? In other words, what appears at first a lyric of moral and spiritual superiority (triumph) over the trials of human experience, becomes finally a revelation of the poet's timorousness in the face of so awesome a metaphysical spectrum as is evoked by death, truth, temptation, judgment. The ambiguity of the syntax conveys the sense of awkward hesitation.

The lyric is composed in common measure, the rimes of its first (*room-overcome*) and last (*pass-countenance*) stanzas imperfect, conveying the unsettling mood of the whole.

I Live with Him, I See His Face (463)

Entitled "Numen Lumen" by its editors when it appeared in *Poems* (1896), the lyric describes the poet's anguished desire for marriage (it is a marriage of spirits, a perpetual presence of the beloved achieved in some mystical union). She and her lover are inseparable, except that death can snatch him from her, forcing upon him the "single privacy" of the grave, his claim (death) outranking hers (marriage). Yet, ironically, the poet concludes, even death cannot separate them, for while she is alive and he is dead, she hears his voice, his presence still here. Such is the mortal witness (the lower way) to immortality, that, the soul departed in death, the relationship of the lovers is "stopless," continuing after death (at least for the living in the haunting memory of the departed), no matter to what judgment the dead have gone.

Perhaps Emily Dickinson is giving mystic and imaginative utterance to a simple and fundamental human experience: that when one we loved very dearly dies, we cannot give up the continual sense of his presence. There are the continual memories, the moments when we catch ourselves turning to ask him some question or to share something with him, a reflexive manifestation of the habit we have so long practiced—then suddenly the realization of death strikes us and makes us feel strange, if also a bit foolish.

The metric pattern is common measure (with elided accented syllables at the ends of lines 3 and 15). The spondaic substitution at the start of line 4 (// x/ x/), joined with the emphasis upon the *d* sound gained from the second syllable of *sundown* (line 3) gives particular force to the word *death,* providing an emphasis appropriate to the sense. Similarly, in the thirteenth line, the trochaic substitution at the start (/x x/ x/ x/), supported by the repetitions of *t* sounds preceding it (*t*oday-*t*o-wi*t*ness-*t*o-cer*t*ain*t*y-immor*t*ali*t*y), thrusts the contrast of immortality and mortality (time) upon us in a striking way (*taught* me by *time*).

(N. B. The want of punctuation presents certain difficulties. There should be a period at the end of line 3, line 4 running into the next stanza. Also, lines 10-13 are a sentence and should be read together, perhaps with only a colon or semi-colon after line 13.)

I Heard a Fly Buzz When I Died (465)

Called "Dying" by its first editors (*Poems,* 1896), the lyric shows Miss Dickinson again taking a stance beyond the grave and writing her own post mortem. The poet seemed always to have been fascinated by the idea of death. When only 21, she had written to Jane Humphrey: "The other day I tried to think how I should look with my eyes shut, and a little white gown on, and a snowdrop on my breast, and I fancied I heard the neighbors stealing in so softly, to look down on my face—so fast asleep—so still." Little more than a decade later, she writes this lyric in which the dead woman recounts her experience of dying, telling how her senses became fixed upon something which sounded like a fly buzzing (she conveys the aural sense very well in her use of sibilants: bu*zz*-*s*tillne*ss*-wa*s*-heave*s*-*s*torm; un*c*ertain-*s*tumbling-bu*zz*-*s*ee-*s*ee).

There is a quality here that will seem to some frivolous: the choice of a common insect to encapsulate the sensation of that significant moment, the eyes wrung dry with weeping, the image of the powerful king (death himself) striding into the room, the enigmatic redundancy which is really not redundant ("and then / I could not see to see")- yet all these are appropriate parts of the imaginative evocation of the intense moment of death. The synaesthesia of the buzz's "blueness," of its uncertain and staggering qualities, of its opacity (shutting out the light) cannot be rationally or logically expounded; yet they fit perfectly into the total vision.

In the first stanza, the inner and outer worlds are merged, the last gasping breaths of the dying becoming the "heaves of storm," perhaps only a metaphor. Death itself is personified as a truculent king entering the room forcibly to carry off his victim. The dying observes all (an ironical circumstance, since commonly it is the living who note the details of the dying man's behavior) until the windows (eyes) fail and obscure the entire scene, the mind fixed upon the fly's buzz.

The stanzaic pattern is that of common measure, all but the last of the rimes imperfect (*room-storm, firm-room, be-fly*). The final agreement (*me-see*) lends a note of resolution, of submission to the strength of death, even perhaps of satisfaction in the final moment of absorption into his kingdom.

I Had No Time To Hate (478)

Much of the lyric's beauty here is derived from its understatement, its want of heroic gesture in talking of two so profound human emotions: hate and love. In essence the poem asserts: "I had time for neither love nor hate, but, since I wanted some 'industry,' I settled to spend my days loving." In each case it is death which aborts the life of love or hate. Life is too brief to spend it in hating (a maxim often heard); one could never finish that task. But Emily Dickinson asserts the opposite is equally true: life is too short to accomplish love's end as well. Yet, having to choose the better of two impossible tasks, she chooses the second, the "little toil of love" as large enough for her to strive after.

While the lyric is arranged into two six-line stanzas, it is clear from the meter and rime that Miss Dickinson has written simply another common measure lyric:

1-2	x/	//	x/	x/
3	x/	x/	x/	
4-5	x/	x/	x/	x/
6	x/	x/	x/	
7-8	x/	x/	x/	x/
9	//	x/	x/	
10-11	x/	x/	x/	x/
12	x/	x/	x/	

The lyric is notably compact, built upon a single rime (*me-enmity-be-me*), constructing two parallel alternatives and selecting the second as her preference.

Going to Him! Happy Letter! (494)

Entitled "The Letter" by its first editors (*Poems,* 1891), the lyric was found in two manuscript forms, a second containing the feminine rather than the masculine pronouns ("Going to her! etc."). It appears to have been written in a state of excitement (or at least is meant to suggest such a state), serving as a defense of her epistolary form. It calls to mind a quite different lyric, one of the loveliest of the English Renaissance: Waller's "Go, Lovely Rose."

In her apostrophe to the letter, she asks it to convey all the things she could not get into writing ("the page I didn't write") and to explain her lapses in syntax (ambiguities are abundant in her elliptical style). She wishes the letter to explain how she rushed over certain passages but moved slowly through others. She even wishes the letter could serve as her spy, to see which passages move the reader deeply.

Further she asks the letter to convey her want of experience in such composition, how desperately she labored in preparing it. But there are some secrets she would not wish revealed; they would be too heart-rending. She asks that he be told how she toiled into the night to try to say what she wished. And the lyric ends with a coy reference to the poet's hiding place for the letter until morning.

Emily Dickinson was an accomplished writer of letters. The three-volume edition of her correspondence is ample testimony. But here she poses as the child, shy yet excited, coy yet exuberant.

While the stanzas are essentially iambic tetrameter octaves (each is very like two long-measure quatrains), the number of substitutions helps to create the agitated state of the speaker's mind:

```
    /x   x/   /x   /x
    /x
    /x   x/   x/   x/
    /x   x/   x/   x/x
 5  x/   x/   xx/  x/
    /x   x/   x/   x/x
    /x   x/   x/   (x)/
    x/   x/   xx/  xx/x(?)
    /x   x/   x/   x/
10  /x   x/   xx/  x/x
    x/   xx/  x/   x/
    xx/  x/   x/   x/x
    x/   x/   xx/  xx/
```

```
      x/   x/   xx/   x/x
15   /x   /x   x/   x/
      x/   x/   x/   x/x
      x/   xx/   x/   x/

      /x   //   xx/   x/x
      xx   //   x/   x/
20   x/   x/   xx/   xx/x(?)
      /x   x/   x/   x/
      /x   x/   x/   x/x
      x/   x/   /x   x/
      x/   x/   x/   x/x
      /x   x/   x/   x/
```

Oddly the second line, while it appears to belong to the first or the third line, except that it would make either a pentameter, defies ordinary prosodic analysis. Yet it does give a clear sense of spontaneity to the impulse. The other substitutions (of trochee and anapest, pyrrhic and spondee, along with a rare and unclassified four-syllable foot, xx/x) create effects of start and stop, of unsureness in the text, all of which suggests a colloquial tone.

I'm Ceded. I've Stopped Being Theirs (508)

Entitled "Love's Baptism" by her first editors (*Poems,* 1890), the lyric is enigmatic and puzzling. The poet enters some new stage of her life, a stage which requires both rejection of her former life and acceptance of some new state of being; it is both a death and a rebirth. Her earliest editors suggest it describes her new found love, that "marriage" which requires that she forsake father and mother and cleave to her "husband." At any rate, she does denounce all familial ties, all the ceremonial remembrances of her former life: her very name, given to her as a child at baptism, is cast off as are the toys of her childhood. That "unwilling" baptism has been precluded by her new, conscious acceptance of grace, her entire being consumed in her new love. Her first estate, the child upon her father's breast (perhaps God is suggested in "Father," but it seems unlikely), is rejected for the second, the woman who has come into her kingdom, her right of womanliness as summed in her choice of love.

The stanza form is unusual in its odd arrangement, the first stanza containing seven lines, three tetrameters, one trimeter, two tetrameter, one trimeter; the second and third stanzas follow a more exact pattern, each containing two tetrameter, one trimeter, two tetrameter, one trimeter sequences. The accentual pattern is irregular at points as well:

	x/	xx	//	x/	a?
	x/	x/	x/	x/	a?
	x/	x/	x/	x/	a?
	x/	x/	x/		b
5	x/	x/	x/	x/	c
	//	/x	x/	x/	c
	x/	x/	x/		b
	/x	x/	x/	x/	d
	x/	//	x/	x/	d
10	x/	x/	x/		e
	/x	x/	x/	x/	f
	x/	xx	//	//	f
	x/	//	x/		e
	x/	x/	//	x/	g
15	//	xx	x/	x/	g
	x/	x/	x/		h
	x/	//	x/	x/	i
	x/	x/	x/	x/	i
	x/	//	x/		h

The clusters of accents in lines 12 and 13 suit the concentration of the elliptical lines, requiring careful pause upon each phrase, just as those of lines 15 and 17 create respective emphasis-contrast and the moment's pause before the choice is made.

The rime scheme (as noted with the scansion above) is regular in pattern, the tetrameter groups riming and the trimeter pairs riming. Most of the rimes, however, are dissonant (the *a*-rime scarcely recognizable as rime, though the words are surely intended to echo one another). The rimes of lines 11 and 12 are arresting, the *d* and *p* sounds shifting about so. Only the rimes of lines 17 and 18 are perfect.

There is an odd syntactic form in line 4: "Is finished using now." We had anticipated: "Is finished being used now" or "I have finished using it now." But Emily Dickinson here as elsewhere prefers the active (*using*) to the passive (*being used*) form, her bent for compression leading her to select the unusual structure (note that the heuristic factor of meter is at work here too, forcing the elliptical form upon her).

It Was Not Death, For I Stood Up (510)

Describing again the emotional crisis of 1862, the poet struggles for the words and images to convey the "chaos" of her mind. While the state had seemed successively like death, night, frost, or fire, as the turmoil took charge of her being, yet her experience was none of these. The one that first catches her imagination is death, the parallels of which she describes in fuller detail. Her very frame calls to mind the bodies she has seen prepared for burial, shrunken, stiff (as if "fitted to a frame"), unable to breathe. Then she elaborates the images of night (a midnight, that moment between yesterday and tomorrow, when time pauses at a timeless instant where days meet) and frost (when the earth, before alive with the heart-beat of abundance, is suddenly taken by death).

We expect her to develop her last simile, that of fire; instead, she surprises us by introducing a new, a less precise, less concrete figure, that of chaos, of a general disorder which appears both endless and hopeless, even beyond the reach of despair.

Most interesting is the pattern of paradox by which the lyric's meaning is developed. In each case, the poet starts by contrast, but ends by affirmation: it wasn't death (all the evidence is against it— I was standing, walking about), yet it "tasted" like what I have imagined death to be (I could imagine myself "set orderly" for burial), etc.

The meter is basically that of common measure (an accented syllable omitted at the end of line 13), though the strong, monosyllabic cadence (especially in the first two stanzas) almost obscures the rhythm:

```
      x/   //   x/   //
      x/   x/   //
      x/   //   x/   x/
      //   x/   x/
 5    x/   //   x/   //
      x/   x/   x/
      //   x/   //   x/
      x/   x/   x/
```

There is a heavy, awesome inexorability in the very rhythm. The same weight is felt in line 18:

```
      x/   //   x/
```

While all but the fifth rimes are imperfect (*down-noon, crawl-cool, seen-mine, frame-some, around-ground, spar-despair*), creating an appropriately disturbed effect, the music of sounds is intricately wrought. In the first stanza, the alliteration (*death-dead, not-night-noon*) is supported by consonance (*it-not-night-put-out, all-bells*). In the second, alliteration of *f* and hard *c* sounds (*frost-for-flesh-felt-fire-for-feet, crawl-could-keep-cool*) add to the general cacophony (an effect repeated in stanzas four through six: *if-life-fitted-frame-frosts-first, could-key-chaos-cool*). Add to that the hissing sibilants of these same stanzas (*some-stopped-space-stares-grisly-frosts-first-morns-most-chaos-stopless-chance-spar-justify-despair*), and we have an unusually effective matching of sound and sense.

If You Were Coming in the Fall (511)

In May of 1862, Wadsworth had left the Arch Street Presbyterian Church in Philadelphia to assume the pastorate of Calvary Church in San Francisco. He had visited Emily Dickinson at Amherst two years earlier. Here the poet appears anxious in not knowing precisely when or if ever he will visit again (of course, the lyric is more general, but its possible biographical meaning is also interesting). It starts in reality and ends in exaggeration or lyric hyperbole. Each statement delays the visit longer (in the fall, in a year, in a few centuries, in eternity) until the sense of distraught emotion is fully realized.

The opening image is casual, the poet shrugging off the period of wait with the nonchalance of a housewife's brushing away a fly. The image of the months swiftly passing is caught in the separate yarn-like balls, put away to keep them from "fusing" in the haste of passage. The child counting off the years by dropping his fingers one by one (Van Dieman is the older name for Tasmania, an island off southeast Australia, likely chosen for its remoteness and romantic potential) has taken us already into the world of fantasy (the dreamlike means of making her sorrow tolerable). The flippant image of life as a rind merely hiding the reality of eternity (a "reality" made possible only in their final meeting there) stretches the imagination beyond belief, destroying altogether any notion of plausibility. Emily Dickinson senses this, for she brings us abruptly back to reality—that she does not know how long it may be before the two meet again (as a point of fact, Wadsworth did visit her again eighteen years later in the summer of 1880). That insistent uncertainty is the goblin bee (the phantom that hovers about us in summer making us think the insect is on us, but which we can't see or feel; it is our minds tormenting us—there is no bee at all).

The meter here is common measure, three of the rimes perfect (*by-fly, hand-land, be-eternity*) and two imperfect (*balls-fuse, between-sting;* significantly the lyric closes with the expectation of rime aborted, leaving us too with the sense of uncertainty). There are skillful echoes of sound (co*m*ing-su*mm*er-brush, *f*or-*f*ear-*f*use, goads-goblin, *st*ate-*st*ing) and syntax (*half a smile, half a spurn*).

The lyric is simply organized, each of the first four stanzas passing a condition of length. While the "logic" is elusive and exaggerated, the simplicity of arrangement gives it a deceptive force of argument.

The Soul Has Bandaged Moments (512)

The lyric has three parts describing (1) the soul's "bandaged" moments, when she is taken captive by fear; (2) the soul's "moments of escape," when she feels a release from all that would make her captive; (3) the soul's "retaken moments" when she lapses again into bandage like a criminal. (It may, of course, be argued that the three parts are actually only two, the third describing the soul's return to its original state.) Written likely in 1862, the lyric is another reflection of the distraught state of Emily Dickinson's mind at the time.

Her soul, paralyzed by fear, is caressed by the "ghastly" goblin (a genuinely evil spirit as viewed in earlier centuries) which replaces the lover's touch (again there may be a suggestion of Wadsworth's departure for California in the lines). For a moment, the soul thinks itself free, dancing carelessly (though the simile of the bomb creates an exaggeratedly sinister image) as does the bee, long-imprisoned and now free to swing from rose to rose. But the "paradise" is only momentary, the "plumed feet" again bound by some new terror which blights its very being.

Emily Dickinson presents her theme in a strikingly dramatic way, showing us the soul's despair, shadowing her moment's exhilaration (creating an effect somewhat akin to the ode of elation in the ancient Greek plays, the joyous choral song which preceded the final calamity), and focusing finally upon the imprisoned "felon."

The stanzaic pattern, while essentially the common meter of the New England hymnal, is set aside for two-line stanzas appearing after the second and fifth quatrains. Actually, the rime would suggest they attach themselves to the quatrains immediately preceding them (*hair-*

o'er-fair; along-song-tongue). The rimes are often slant, creating an appropriate dissonance of sound which substantiates the gloom of the lines.

Throughout the lyric there are effective examples of poetic devices: internal rime in line 8 (*lover-hovered*), assonance (h*a*s-b*a*ndaged in line 1; sh*e*-f*ee*ls in line 3; s*ou*l-m*o*ments in stanza four; kn*o*w-n*o*-m*o*re in stanza five), and alliteration (*f*eels-*f*right-*f*ingers-*f*reezing-*f*rom-*f*air, *s*top-*s*alute-*s*ip-*s*oul, and *th*ought-*th*eme in stanzas one through three; *b*ursting-*b*omb-*b*ee-*b*orne, *d*oors-*d*ances-*d*o-*d*elirious-*d*ungeoned, and *kn*ow-*n*o-*n*oon in stanzas four and five; *f*elon-*f*eet, *s*oul-*s*taples-*s*ong, and *h*orror-*h*er in stanzas six and seven).

I Started Early—Took My Dog (520)

Entitled "By the Sea" by her editors (*Poems,* 1891), the lyric appears at first to record a simple experience, the poet walking along the shore with her dog. She describes the sea in shifting metaphor, first as a house (the mythic mermaids ascending from the "basement," the ships afloat on an "upper floor"), then as a living human (?) creature who assaults the poet with his mighty force (the tide moving inland upon her, intent upon devouring her until she is safe again in town—the tide, an embarrassed and dignified, if somewhat too zealous, lover, recedes). (Note: the closing image of the lyric has led some, Clark Griffith for example, to see in the lyric a covert picture of the poet's apprehension about the sexual experience, a preoccupation of her mind related somehow to her "love" for Wadsworth, the shoe filled with pearl suggesting the actual coition.)

The stanzaic pattern is that of common measure (an accented syllable elided from line 3). It moves with the swiftness of lyric simplicity until slowed by the cluster of accents in line 9:

x/ // x/ x/.

The pattern is broken again in line 17 when the poet stammers momentarily:

x/ // x/ x/.

The effect is that her calmness at the shore is exchanged by the momentary terror of the sea's pursuit (now personified as the rapacious villain set upon possessing the frightened girl). But she escapes him in the daylight company of her townspeople; the sea quietly withdraws.

The rimes are, at the start, perfect, matching the morning calm of the beachstroller. The final two are imperfect, sharing the maid's unsettled state. There are striking effects of alliteration (*m*ermaid-*m*e-*m*ouse-*m*an-*m*oved-*m*e and *t*ill-*t*ide in stanzas one through three; *f*rigates-*f*loor and *h*empen-*h*ands in stanza two; *b*elt-*b*odice in stanza three; *d*ew-*d*andelion in stanza four; *h*e-*h*e-*h*is-*h*eel in stanza five; *s*olid-*s*eemed-*s*ea in stanza six; note too that there is at least one major *s* sound in each stanza: *s*tarted-*s*ea, *s*ands, *s*imple, *s*leeve-*s*tarted, *s*ilver, *s*olid-*s*ea) and assonance (b*a*sement-c*a*me in stanza one; ex-tended-h*e*mpen, m*e*-b*e*, and m*ou*se-agr*ou*nd in stanza two; h*e*-*e*at-m*e*-sl*ee*ve in stanza four).

To Hear an Oriole Sing (526)

Entitled "The Oriole's Secret" by its first editors (*Poems,* 1891), the lyric presents a common theme: that so often two people respond differently to the same stimulus (in this case the oriole's song). Some hear the song and think it only common, dun, or not at all poetical; others hear the same tune and find it divine, fair, and rune (poetical). Why such varied responses? The answer lies within the listener; he makes of the song what he will. The song is not "in the tree," not simply the product of the bird's singing; it is "in thee," it is the soul's recreation of beauty or indifference.

There are a number of striking effects of language. For example, the placing of "only" before *divine* is arresting: is it meant to imply that the oriole's song is "only divine," or is the understatement calculated for emphasis? There is too the unusual shift of prepositions in stanza two. "It (the paradoxical effect) is not of the bird . . . (so much as it is attributable) unto (the) crowd (which listens)"; in either case (whether his song is judged common or divine), the bird sings as he would even if his song were unheard. The listener's ear "attireth" (clothes) the song with a fair or dun garment. The word *rune* is archaic, giving a note of remote fantasy to the lyric, contrasted sharply with its opposite (*none*).

The metric pattern is unusual for Miss Dickinson. Generally the first two lines of the three-line stanza are iambic trimeter, the third line iambic dimeter (except that the third line of the first stanza is iambic trimeter as well). The rimes are oddly organized also, the first two lines riming perfectly (except for *rune-none* in stanza four), while the third in each case startles us by its imperfect attachment (an effect supported too by the abrupt start of the shortened meter). This reduction of the lines to dimeter may add as well a note of conviction, of finality on the poet's part—she determined to have her own way about it.

Mine by the Right of the White Election (528)

Entitled "Mine" by its earliest editors (*Poems,* 1890), the lyric is perplexing as to meaning. Many of its images are Biblical: the elect, robed in the white garments of salvation, the royal seal of Revelation's scroll, the prison of Hades into which Christ descended to lead "captivity captive," the visionary nature of the experience, the hint of resurrection ("the grave's repeal"). The speaker may even be thought to be Christ or God, declaring the redeemed His possession throughout eternity. However, some see it as alluding to Emily Dickinson's "marriage," her "election" of the single soul who is to share her life and love, the two of them one throughout eternity by her sovereign choice. At any rate, it is a difficult lyric.

The meter, while irregular, falls essentially into the pattern of common measure (and is built upon the single perfect rime *seal-conceal-repeal-steal*). The seventh and eighth lines are actually one, the third of the second stanza:

```
    /xx  /x   x/   x/x
    /x   x/   x/
    /xx  /x   x/   x/x
   (x)/  x/   x/
 5  //   x/   xx   x/x
    /x   x/   x/
    /x   x/
              x/x   x/x
    //   x/   x/
```

In each case, the *mine* converts the iambic foot to trochaic (2, 4?, 6), spondaic (5, 9), or dactyllic (1, 3), stressing the quality of possessiveness which pervades the sense.

The assonance (m*i*ne-b*y*-r*i*ght-wh*i*te, m*i*ne-b*y*-s*i*gn, sc*a*rlet-b*a*rs), alliteration (*r*ight-*r*oyal-*r*epeal, *s*eal-*s*ign-*s*carlet-*s*teal, *c*annot-*c*onceal-*c*onfirmed, *v*ision-*v*eto), and consonance (righ*t*-whi*t*e, roya*l*-sea*l*, sig*n*-priso*n*, mi*n*e-i*n*-visio*n*-a*n*d-i*n*) create musical echoes which give the lyric part of its charm.

I'm Sorry for the Dead Today (529)

It's haying time, one of the pleasant seasons of the New England year, and Emily Dickinson thinks of the dead, wondering if they do not feel "lonesome" especially now, longing to join the living. At haying the neighbors converse over the fence; acquaintances pause in their labors to talk and laugh (so heartily that the fences themselves share in their frivolity). In contrast, the dead lie buried in the quiet of their graves (she uses *straight* in its obsolete sense of arduous, difficult, or trying). The poet feels "a trouble," a concern that the dead may be "homesick" for their loved ones, especially at haying time.

The stanzaic pattern is the common measure (though accented syllables are elided in lines 3, 5, 7, 13, 15), the second and fourth lines riming (though in the first stanza it is the first and fourth; note also the slight jar given by the slant rimes of stanzas two and three). The tone of the whole is serious, the lively images of haying setting off the general sobriety in an interesting way.

A number of unusual syntactic forms mark the lyric: for example, "acquaintance discourse" gives us a start in its failure of agreement (unless the subjunctive is intended); the same effect is found in "sepulchre don't," as though the totality of graves is wrapped into the single noun.

In addition, there are several instances of compression, as, for example, in the implied *when* at the start of line 4. Some such phrase as *of laughter* is omitted at the end of line 7 and *I feel* at the start of line 13 (*I feel troubled* had been the more normal phrase, just as *I wonder* had been for line 17). And, in line 17, what is actually meant is "(I) wonder if (those in the) sepulchre / Don't feel a lonesome way" (where "feel lonesome" had been better prose, the awkward phrase apparently required in the meter).

The Heart Asks Pleasure First (536)

Here Emily Dickinson constructs an order of the heart's preferences: if at all possible, the heart would prefer pleasure; if not, then simply to be free of pain; that wish denied, it would request some pain killer (an anodyne) to keep it from suffering; and that too impossible, the heart asks to be put to sleep, to be rendered unconscious so that it knows nothing of the body's anguish; and finally, if all else is denied, the heart asks its Inquisitor (the disease? God?) to be allowed to die. The brief lyric's strength lies in its compactness, its unadorned sincerity, enunciating its successive preferences in the simplest, most direct way (note the *first, and then, and then,* etc., arrangement).

The metric pattern is that of the short meter, the three short trimeter lines (1, 2, and 4 of each stanza) allowing the poet to state her intention succinctly, without the slightest exaggeration, without any heroics whatever. The longer third line (iambic tetrameter), however, keeps the lyric from a monotonous sing-song (note how the pauses after each *and then* give the reader a moment to absorb the meaning). The rimes are appropriately dissonant, failing to satisfy expectation and creating the tension necessary in the meaning. Because the lyric is so brief, the alliteration of *pleasure-pain* is heard again in *privilege,* and *dead* is caught by the mind in *die* (the semantic attraction of the two words is also important, just as the antonymical relation of *pleasure* and *pain* in the earlier example increases the association). *Suffering* and *sleep* as well echo one another alliteratively.

I've Seen a Dying Eye (547)

Here again Emily Dickinson's fascination with death, especially with the details of it, is evident. What is it like to die? She focusses upon that strange phenomenon that so often accompanies death: with a kind of fear the dying look desperately about the room, as if in search of something, as if wanting to see some particular person, as if to give some message before departing. Often the searching eye is not satisfied, but clouds and closes (*soldered down*—as if it were impossible to separate the lids again), without ever making us aware of what it has seen or what it had sought. Miss Dickinson, in this instance, imagines the "dying eye" as having some blessed vision at the moment of demise, a vision that the living would love to have seen.

While the lyric often appears as a single eight-line stanza, it is clear that Miss Dickinson intended it to be two stanzas composed in short measure (she avoids the pitfalls of the stanza form, its tendency toward sing-song, by the pauses in the second stanza, *and then—,* and by the slight start given us in the slant rimes: *room-become, down-seen*). The alliteration (*seen-search-something-seemed-soldered-seen, run-round-round-room,* and *dying-down-disclosing*), assonance (*I've-*

dying-*eye* and fog-s*o*ldered) and consonance (see*n*-ru*n*-the*n*-down-
see*n* and roo*m*-so*m*ething-see*m*ed-beco*m*e), show a care in composition of the lines.

That I Did Always Love (549)

The lover's proof of her love is the theme of this lyric, entitled
"Proof" by its first editors (*Poems,* 1890). The first stanza turns to
the lover's history ("That I *did* always love"), the second to her
future ("That I *shall* love alway"). In the first argument the evidence
is that loving and living are one and that the lover had no sufficient
life until she loved (thus before she was "born" to love, she was not
really alive). In the second argument, the evidence is the same: love
is life, and life is immortal; therefore her love is everlasting.

And what if her lover will not believe her? Then she can only
point to Calvary, the supreme symbol of live—its laying down its
life in suffering and selflessness. The allusion doubtless touches us
as hyperbole; yet Emily Dickinson did suffer great anguish and the
torture of self-denial in her love (if Wadsworth is meant). In effect
she argues: would I have endured such suffering (a Calvary of woe)
if my love for you had not been so invincibly durable?

The stanzaic meters here are each unique, built primarily on two-
and three-foot lines (with a single tetrameter):

```
      x/  x/  x/
      x/  x/
      x/  x/
      x/  x/  x/
  5   x/  x/  //
      x/  x/
      x/  x/
      x/  x/  x/  x/

      /xx  //
 10   (x)/  x/
      /x  x/
      x/  x/
```

The words become in each case their own metric law, and while the
beat is essentially iambic, there are slow, provocative spondees
(lines 5 and 9) and an apparent dactyl (line 9).

The first and last rimes are typically slant (*proof-enough, I-Calvary*), conveying the bewilderment of the poet's mind. There are plays upon words (*always-alway, loved-lived, love-life*) and striking phonetic effects (ti*ll-I-loved-I*-never-*lived*, love-is-*life*-and-*life*, *dost*-doub*t*-*s*wee*t*).

I Measure Every Grief I Meet (561)

Emily Dickinson was singularly sensitive to pain, not merely her own, but that of those she loved. Suffering half-frightened, half-fascinated her. She had known pain, especially the anguish of mind which struck her in the psychic depression she experienced in 1862. In this lyric, entitled "Griefs" by her first editors, she shows an almost analytic curiosity about human suffering. Most of us turn eagerly from grief; Miss Dickinson turns toward it. She probes the nature of grief and pain in her fellows, all in an effort to comprehend it in herself. She asks unusual questions, questions which seem to have no answers. How heavy is "their" grief as compared to mine? Have they borne theirs longer than I have mine? Does their grief ever become so intense that they feel they cannot go on living? Can the passage of years provide a balm for their grief, or will they grieve for "centuries of nerve"?

The last stanzas are a catalogue of grief and its causes: death, want, cold, despair, banishment. These are the "fashions of the cross" which the poet explores to find if others suffer as she does and, in that common bond of human grief, to find comfort. In conclusion, she invokes the supreme human suffering, the passion of Christ. She does so in an utterly muted voice, arriving there as the climactic emblem of trial and grief.

The fourth line surprises us by its choice of *easier:* we had anticipated *heavier* or *lighter* to suit the implication of *weighs* (yet *easier* implies *lighter,* while it also focusses semantically on *ease* in contrast to *difficulty*). The choice gives us double mileage in suggesting the more obvious meaning, while actually extending the sense to take in a new idea.

The last stanza contains an ambiguity in the line "And how they're mostly worn," suggesting either: (1) that she wonders just how the suffering "wear" their cross or (2) that there is a publicity in the bearing of a cross, an ostentation by which what should be private becomes public.

The meter of the lyric is common measure, the rimes mixed between perfect (*eyes-size, try-die, despair-air, me-Calvary*) and imperfect (*begin-pain, smile-oil, harm-balm, nerve-love, cause-eyes, worn-own*). It is one of Emily Dickinson's longest poems, and perhaps the need for the perfect rimes to set the stanzas in motion is created as much by the length as by anything else. But these perfect rimes only single out the imperfect ones and their effect of dissonance more decidedly.

While her use of poetic devices is not so prominent as in other of her lyrics, there are numerous examples of alliteration (*w*ith-*w*onder-*w*eighs in stanza one; *s*ome-*s*mile and *l*ong-*l*ength-*l*ight in stanza four; *h*arm-*h*urt in stanza five; *k*ind-*c*orrectly-*c*omfort-*C*alvary-*c*ross and *p*iercing-*p*assing in stanzas nine and ten), assonance (m*ea*sure-*e*very and gr*ie*f-m*ee*t in stanza one; h*u*rt-*ea*rly in stanza five; b*u*t-*o*ne-c*o*mes-b*u*t-*o*nce in stanza seven), and consonance (measure-every-grief-narrow-probing and measure-eyes-weighs-has-easier-size in stanza one; com*f*ort a*ff*ords-*f*ashions-*f*ascinated and pre*s*ume-*s*ome-*m*y in stanzas nine and ten).

My Period Had Come for Prayer (564)

In this lyric of that crisis year 1862, the poet approaches God in prayer, all of her other means spent, her strategies all having failed; but so awed is she by His infinite and mysterious being she cannot bring her finite request to Him, but can only worship Him. In the first stanza, she even speculates that it may have been God, the Creator Himself, who caused her plans to fail so utterly that she was driven to Him. Yet, when she seeks His presence, with hyperbole of description she steps upon the vast stretches of the north to meet with her "Friend." There is no tangible sign of Him anywhere, no dwelling, no address, only the prairie-like expanse of space (air). She asks whether God has no "face," no palpable being by which to comfort the quester. She is answered only in silence. For a moment, the creation itself pauses in reverence to so infinite a being. Forgetting her errand (awed beyond it), she worships Him.

The lyric is not so highly polished as are some of those of the same period, but it is nonetheless provocative in its rougher state. The metric pattern is that of common measure (note the three syllables suggested by *prairies* [/x/] in line 12; also, the elision of accented feet at the ends of lines 13, 17, and 19 creates the necessity of a pause which in turn enhances the meditative mood of the lines). There are curious effects of alliteration (*p*eriod-*p*rayer in stanza one, *G*od-*g*rows and *s*o-*s*tepped-*s*ee in stanza two; *H*is-*h*ouse-*h*ad-*h*e in stanza three; *s*ilence-*s*topped and *c*ondescended-*c*reation in stanza five), assonance (gr*o*ws-th*o*se in stanza two; n*o*r-d*oo*r and pr*ai*ries-*ai*r in stanza three; *I*-m*i*ght-s*i*lence in stanzas four and five), and consonance (mu*st*-a*s*cend-*so*-*st*epped-*s*ee-thi*s*-curiou*s* in stanza two; *s*ilen*c*e-*c*onde*sc*en-d*ed*-*c*reation-*s*topped in stanza five).

We Learned the Whole of Love (568)

Written in the year of Wadsworth's departure for California, this lyric tempts us to speculate upon its relation to him. Emily Dickinson testifies in her poems that she loved deeply. Perhaps she did, perhaps only as those who have loved and lost can love, with an intensity of desire which can never be fulfilled in the reality of the lovers' touch. Here she sees her love completely fulfilled, building the sense upon the paradox that, while she has "learned the whole of love," she realizes she is only a child in comprehension of its infinite truth and wisdom.

The lyric is notable for its simplicity, its straightforward figure of love's progress, like a child's comprehension of the art of reading: he learns first the alphabet, then words, then the short chapter, until at last he can comprehend the entire volume (there may be suggested here various "stages" of love from that first moment of contact to the consummation of love in the sexual relation; however, that surely is only a part of the meaning). Yet, having attained so much, each of the lovers must face the other with the child's naïveté, not really comprehending what he/she has experienced.

The stanzaic pattern here is that of short measure, the dissonance of the rimes conveying the quiet bewilderment of the lovers in the incomprehensibility of their love. The large number of pauses required by the meaning and arrangement of the lines creates a proper feeling of awe in the metaphorical recital of the history of their love. The few poetic echoes (*l*earned-who*l*e-*l*ove, *ch*apter-ea*ch*-*ch*ildhood's-ea*ch*-*ch*ild, etc.) give the lyric a phonetic coherence which has an interest of its own.

I Like To See It Lap the Miles (585)

Miss Dickinson has built this lyric upon the metaphor of the horse, which, in the distracting progress of the day, was being rapidly replaced by the "iron horse" of her own generation (it was entitled "The Railway Train" by its first editors, *Poems,* 1891). The punctual engine, arriving at its destination with a chronological precision like that of the stars (an assertion with which the modern traveller is likely to disagree; Miss Dickinson may have intended only a mild humor in it), the vivid landscape past which the train runs—through valleys, past storage tanks and quarries, in tunnels, and down steep inclines—both are described in such a way as to impress them upon the senses.

The lyric creates a sense of breathless and continual motion, there being no pauses at the ends of stanzas. We do slow down at the conclusion of the third stanza, but we halt only when we reach the word "stop," pausing to see the paradox of the train's docility alongside its seeming omnipotence (it is at once under control and all-powerful in its own energy). But the poem does not move with uniform speed across the countryside: we are forced to linger over the relatively abstruse words of the first two stanzas and the allusion of the last stanza ("prodigious," "supercilious," "Boanerges"); yet we dare not labor these intellectualisms either, or they will destroy the sense of childlike wonder in the lines. Other moments of hesitation too are the result of accented syllables omitted at the ends of lines (e. g., line 5—x/ x/ x/ x). Mentally we fill out the omission in a momentary pause, holding back just slightly the rapid onrush of the locomotive.

Most absorbing here too is the interaction of semantic (meaning) and phonological (sound) elements. The *l, p,* and *f* sounds, which dominate parts of the lyric, support the licking, lapping, and puffing intended as the train moves along. The onomatopoetic effects (the imitation of meaning in the sounds of the words) of the *horrid-hooting* and *neigh-Boanerges* add a quality of delight to the aural (sound) imagery.

There are too remarkable cacophonous (harsh-sounding) effects suitable to the noise of the train. Note, for example, the dissonant rimes (*up-step, peer-pare, while-hill, star-door*) in each stanza, frustrating our expectation that the sounds will be more perfectly matched. Note too how the increase of harsh sounds in the tunnel is supported in the very words of the third stanza.

The formal arrangement is a rather regular ballad stanza (though in some editions the third stanza is grouped into five lines), tetrameter, trimeter, tetrameter, trimeter, in iambic feet and riming *abcb* (also called common measure). The subtleties of metrical variants aid the general effect. For example, the spondaic ending of the last line of stanza three (x/ x/ //) stretches the line so that we can actually see the long row of boxcars chasing one another.

There is a subtle and intricate balance too in the last two lines of the lyric, the spondee and pyrrhic of the next-to-the-last line balancing off the pyrrhic and spondee of the last line:

```
//  xx  x/  x/
xx  //  x/
```

The order of the spondee and pyrrhic emphasizes the sudden change from continual motion to standstill. The order of the pyrrhic and spondee gives stress to the word "own"—the train cannot lose its way, bound as it is to its *own* tracks.

Three Times We Parted—Breath and I (598)

Building her lyric upon the analogy we often hear of the drowning (that one can come up three times from the water, but that he will not rise a fourth), Emily Dickinson alludes to three experiences so devastating they were like death, like three partings with breath (the metaphor of life). The sense of desperation in which the breath strives to return to the lungs ("the lifeless fan") is conveyed in the first stanza. Like a plaything to the fierce waves, she is tossed about by the same billows which carry off the ship she strives toward (longing to die at least with the sail in view, since it bespeaks of human life for her).

At the moment she is ready to give up life, however, the dawn arrives and she is spared. The storm has subsided; death that had swallowed her up (in the image of the chrysalis) is kissed by the sun, and she is risen to renewed life (it is possible to see here a hint of ritual in the triple baptism in the name of Father, Son, and Spirit—the sacrament of death and life).

The meter is that of common measure, the rimes dissonant throughout, showing the agitated state of the poet's mind. Alliteration (*strove-stir-strove-stay* in stanza one, *billows-ball-blue* in stanza two, *leagues-liked-like-lulled-lived*, *waves-winds*, *sunrise-stood*, and *kissed-chrysalis* in stanzas three and four) plays a major part in the phonetic organization of the lines.

I Years Had Been from Home (609)

Called "Returning" by its first editors (*Poems,* 1891), the lyric dramatizes one's return to her home after years of absence, only to find she dares not enter her former dwelling. The whole is apparently metaphorical, speaking actually of the poet's return to her former life, some "business" of living she had left behind and wished to claim again. She cannot return, for she fears the unfamiliar, unknown face that may have usurped her dwelling. In awe of the present fear, her mind wanders back to the life she had known there ("before")— it rushes in upon her like a flood, overwhelming her utterly.

She had courageously faced consternation since leaving that door, and she laughs a nervous laugh at her present fear. She takes hold of the latch as if her courage had been restored, but lets it go as cautiously as she had taken it, running frantically from the unopened door.

The lines are very near allegory, suggesting the frequent human desire to take up a part of life long ago deserted, to meet again friends we had once known or been intimate with. Often we believe we have not changed at all with the passing years and that we can pick up life at that earlier moment and resume it. But usually, if we try, we discover the passage of time has made such a return impossible—we cannot recover those parts of our lives left behind.

The metric pattern is that of short measure (there being an accented syllable elided from line 15). Interestingly, all but the final stanza's rimes contain the *r* sound (door-before, there-there, before-ear, door-before, care-floor), creating the echoing effect and hinting that all the stanzas are one; the final rime (*glass-house*) startles us both by its deviation from the pattern and by its dissonance. Alliteration (*d*oor-*d*ared in stanza one; *s*aw-*s*tare-*s*tolid in stanza two; *l*ife-*l*eft-*l*eaned-*l*ingered-*l*ike-*l*aughed and *b*usiness-*b*efore-*b*roke in stanzas two through four; *c*rumbling-*c*ould-*c*onsternation-*c*ompassed in stanza four, *f*ear-*f*itted-*f*loor-*f*ingers-*f*led and *g*lass-*g*asping in stanzas four through six), assonance (*e*nter-l*e*st-n*e*ver in stanza one; *o*cean-r*o*lled-br*o*ke in stanza three; l*a*tch-h*a*nd, tr*e*mbling-l*e*st, and l*ea*ve-m*e* in stanza five; *a*s-gl*a*ss in stanza six), and consonance (f*r*om-ho*m*e, be*f*o*r*e-*d*oo*r*-*d*a*r*ed-ente*r* and le*s*t-*f*a*c*e-*s*aw [catching the alliteration of sibilants in stanza two] in stanza one; l*ea*ned-l*i*nge*r*ed-*s*econd-*r*olled in stanza three; lau*gh*ed-lau*gh*-*f*ear-be*f*ore and con*s*ter*n*ation-com-pa*ss*ed-win*ced* in stanza four) play central roles in the phonetic scheme.

Our Journey Had Advanced (615)

Entitled "The Journey" by her earliest editors (*Poems,* 1891), the lyric describes the moment of death at the end of a long journey, the soul reluctant as it approaches "that odd fork in being's road," but swept into the ecstasy of assurance in its vision of God at every gate. The start of the lines is inconspicuous, focussing on what seems a temporal journey, but coming abruptly upon the mystical images of eternity. At first the soul is fearful, reluctant, terrified by the "forest of the dead" which lies just ahead. But, having no hope of retreat, the soul turns stoically to face the reality, only to have its vision of God at every gate.

The meter is again that of short measure, the brief trimeters lending a matter-of-fact tone to the whole, allowing the short, almost abrupt emphasis of the three stresses per line; the tetrameters, however, destroy the potential monotony of the briefer lines. Above the iambic meter too come the moments of hesitation, as in the spondee of the third line (x/ // x/ x/), giving the reader opportunity to assimilate the quality of strangeness implied in the sense. The same reluctance is reflected in the meter of the fifth line (x/ // x/), and an emphasis is gained in the eleventh for the white flag of eternity (x/ x/ // x/). The alliterative echoes (note how *before-between-behind* in stanzas two and three stresses the relationship, semantic as well as syntactic; *retreat-route* again in stanza three have a semantic as well as a phonetic attraction; *God-gate* in the final line creates an emphasis appropriate to the meaning; *feet-fork-feet-forest-flag* stretch throughout the lyric, giving a sense of unity [created in sound] to the whole) are supplemented by other special effects (such as the dissonant rimes of stanzas one and three and the echo-like effects of *odd-road* in line three and *eternity-term* in line four).

'Twas a Long Parting (625)

Entitled "Resurrection" by its earliest editors (*Poems,* 1890), the lyric describes the meeting at God's judgment bar of two earthly lovers. They have come to be "interviewed," to give account to Him for their lives upon earth. Yet, ironically, their attention is not fixed on Him, but on one another, meeting again as celestial lovers. The "fleshless" may be meant to suggest not only that this second meeting is in eternity where they stand bodiless, but it may speak as well of the "Platonic" quality of their temporal love (if Wadsworth is meant, the implication is likely the latter). Now, as they stand in eternity, they are not hindered by a threat of "lifetime," the short span of years which can destroy the lovers. They are in the same state as the unborn soul, except that their "birth" (resurrection) has made them now infinite.

Perhaps in the last stanza Emily Dickinson alludes to the marriage supper of the Lamb and His Bride (the church) described in Revelation XIX. There the wedding of Christ and His risen saints is seen as the opening event of rejoicing in eternity. But in Emily Dickinson's vision, she and her lover (the Rev. Wadsworth?) are honored members of the wedding, paradise their host, and the cherubs and seraphs their bridal guests.

The metric pattern of the lyric shifts, stanza one written in common measure (though the first line is irregular, laying stress upon the length of separation: xx // xx x/), while the rest of the lyric is in short measure (except that there is a loss of syllable in line 9, a loss compensated for by the heavy stress of the line: // // x?). All the rimes are dissonant (*come-time, gaze-eyes, new-now, host-guest*), conveying the quality of strangeness perhaps in the speculated confrontation of lovers in the presence of God. (Note how the alliteration of *b* sounds in the final stanzas [*beheld-born-bridal*] builds to the stress of *bridal*.)

The Lightning Playeth All the While (630)

Another of Emily Dickinson's "nature" poems, this lyric describes the lightning, centering at first upon the paradox of its playfulness as contrasted with its enormous destructive power. Then, in the middle of the second stanza, the contrast shifts to that between the terrifying lightning and the harmless passage of the same electrical power through the "ropes" (wires) above our heads (we scarcely react to that continual flow of electrical force, but the lightning inspires awe and respect in us).

The metric pattern of the lyric is that of common measure, the rimes appropriately dissonant (conveying the want of ease at the thought of so great a power). Note too the dominance of sibilant sounds which create a cacophonous effect (*singeth-ourselves-conscious-exist-stern-insulators-whose-short-sepulchral-bass-alarms-us-his-pass-counterpass-ropes-news-so-much-check-speech-stop-cross-ourselves*).

The Brain Is Wider Than the Sky (632)

Entitled "The Brain" by its earliest editors (*Poems*, 1896), the lyric speaks not of the brain as a physical organ, but of the mind or soul housed in the brain. Its argument of the infinity and superiority of the brain is made by comparison: the mind is wider (can comprehend more fully?) than the sky; it can assimilate the heavens and still have room. The mind is deeper (capable of more profundity, depth?) than the sea; like a sponge, the mind can absorb the sea. The mind (soul) is like God, for He is spirit too, unfettered by the finite limits of space and time; whatever difference there be (in substance at least), it is slight.

The lyric is a perfectly regular example of common measure (with the possible exception that *side-beside* in stanza one are not true examples of rime, but of repetition). It has a remarkable quality of assurance in its steady fulfillment of expectation both in rhythm and in rime. It might have become monotonously sing-song under those circumstances, but Emily Dickinson avoids the danger by requiring pauses within lines (e. g., after "ease" in line 4, "them" in 6 and 10, and "differ" in 11) and a slower pace at various points (e. g., "sponges buckets," a retardation of tempo demanded in the clusters of consonant sounds; "the one the other," a slowing down required by the mind to absorb the meaning). The alliteration of *b* and *s* sounds ties the lyric together phonetically in an unusual way (*b*rain-*b*eside-*b*rain-*b*lue-*b*uckets-*b*rain; *s*ky-*s*ide-*s*ea-*s*ponges-*s*yllable-*s*ound).

The Way I Read a Letter's This (636)

In this lyric Emily Dickinson's love of privacy, her shyness in all things, is evident. Even when she reads a letter, she secludes herself, locking the door of her room, trying it to be sure it is fast, withdrawing so far she cannot even hear a knock—and then she opens the letter, meditating upon it in quiet exhilaration (it is an ambiguity of the lines that we do not know for certain whether it is the poet or the mouse that has stolen into the room to peruse her infiniteness and sigh for lack of such bliss, such a "heaven"—the sense appears to favor the mouse's awe at the poet's ecstasy).

The metric pattern is that of common measure, the rimes (after the first stanza) perfect, giving the sense of satisfaction and excitement in the stealthy bliss of her received epistle. The alliteration of *f* sounds (*f*irst-*f*ingers-*f*or-*f*urthest-*f*orth-*f*loor-*f*or-*f*irm) is supported consonantally at several points (o*f*f-be*f*ore-in*f*inite), just as the alliteration of *l* sounds (*l*etter-*l*ock-*l*ittle-*l*etter-*l*ock-*l*ack) is also supported consonantally (s*l*owly-g*l*ancing-wa*ll*-f*l*oor). Note too the interest created consonantally by the echoed *k* sounds throughout (lo*ck*-ne*x*t-*c*ounteract-kno*ck*-pi*ck*-lo*ck*-*c*onviction-e*x*orcised-la*ck*).

I Cannot Live with You (640)

Entitled "In Vain" by its earliest editors (*Poems,* 1890), the lyric conveys the poet's determined sense of hopelessness in her love for the Rev. Wadsworth: she can neither live nor die nor rise with him, but their love must exist "oceans" apart. In each case, she presents a drama of her view. She cannot live with him, for her life is like a piece of broken porcelain shut up in a cupboard by the sexton (God?); she is emotionally broken, incapable of meeting the demands of "life" with him.

Nor could she die with him (at the end of their "lives" together). She knows that he could never face her dying before him, and she could not endure his death (the shutting of the gaze down, the closing of the corpse's eyes in death; the frost of the body growing cold) without dying herself at the same time.

And she certainly could not meet him in resurrection, for fear her love of him would utterly destroy her love of Jesus. She knows she would always make him her lord, preferring his presence to Christ's. By what standard could the lovers be judged in eternity? "You" (surely the Rev. Wadsworth is intended) "served heaven," while I made you the object of my idolatry. If you were lost (among the damned), I would insist that I be too though I were declared the greatest saint of heaven; if you were saved (among the redeemed) and I not allowed to stand at your side, that would be a hell of separation.

The conclusion? Since we cannot love in life, death, or resurrection, we must "meet apart," lovers separated by oceans, prayer, and despair (the "white" sustainer of their love). Written the year of Wadsworth's departure for California, the lyric is one of the clearest declarations of Emily Dickinson's feeling for him.

The meter is odd and irregular at many points, suggesting emphatically the distraught state of the poet's mind in that year of emotional crisis (1862):

```
    //   x/   x/
    x/   x/                    life
    x/   x/   x/
    x/   x/                    shelf
 5  x/   x/   x/   x
     /   x/                    up
    //   //   x/
    (x)/  x/                   cup

    x/   x/   x/   x
10   /   x/                    broke
    x/   x/  (x)/   x
     /   x/                    crack

    x/   x/   x/
    x/   x/                    wait
15  x/   x/   x/   /
     /   x/                    not

    x/   x/   //
    x/   //                    freeze
    x/   x/   x/
20  //   x/                    privilege

    x/   x/   x/
    x/   //                    face
    x/   x/   xx?
    (x)x  //                   grace

25  //   x/   x
     x   x/   //               eye
    x/   x/   x/
    //   x/                    by

    //   x/
30  x/   //   x/               know
    x/   x
     /   x/                    not

    x/   //   x/   x/
    x/   x/   //               eyes
35  x/   x/   x/
    x/   x/                    paradise
```

```
        x/   //   /x , /
         x   //                    name
         //  x
40       x  x/   xx/               fame

        x/   //
        x/  x/   x/                be
        x/  x/
        //  x/   x/                me

45      x/  x/   x/
        //   //                    here
        x/  x/   x/
        x/  x/   x/                prayer
        x/  //   x/
50      x/                         despair
```

The meter has in it a number of spondees, weighing down the lines to give the quality of despair the poet is striving after (e. g., *our life—his porcelain* in line 7, *you freeze* in line 18, *death's privilege* in line 20; *your face* in line 22; *new grace, glow plain* in lines 24-25; *you there —I here* in line 46; etc.). The total effect of the apparent metric disorder is to give a prose-like urgency and significance to the lines, as though the poet must destroy the shackles of meter to attain her sense.

The rimes are difficult for the ear to discern at times (as in stanzas one, three, four, five, and especially eight), though they are obvious at other points (stanzas two, six, seven, nine, ten, eleven, and twelve). Perhaps there are more perfect rimes than usual in such a Dickinson lyric to offset the bewildering irregularity of the meter. The lyric plays upon words and meanings (e. g., *live-life* in stanzas one and two, and the paradox of *meet* and *apart* in the final stanza). The strong alliterative effects (e. g., *p*utting-*p*orcelain-*p*leases in stanzas two and three; *f*reeze-*f*rost-*f*ace-*f*oreign in stanzas five through seven, *s*erved-*s*ought-*s*aturated-*s*ight-*s*ordid-*s*aved-*s*elf-*s*o-*s*ustenance in stanzas eight through twelve) are supplemented by other kinds of echoes (e. g., *keeps the key* in line 5; the consonantal *r* sound in the last stanza: apa*r*t-the*r*e-he*r*e-doo*r*-aja*r*-a*r*e-p*r*aye*r*-despai*r*).

Pain Has an Element of Blank (650)

Entitled "The Mystery of Pain" by its earliest editors (*Poems,* 1890), this brief lyric aims at defining the experience of pain—not so much to tell us what pain is like, but to speak of it as it relates to time. Pain exists outside the temporal experience completely. It has an element of temporal "blankness." It cannot date itself as to its start (it seems always to have been); nor can it relate to past and future: it is only infinitely *now* in experience. So infinite is pain that it cannot reckon with past or future, but only experiences the present and new periods of pain.

There are a number of awkward and ambiguous syntactic forms in the lyric (perhaps intended to convey the confused state of the suffering mind). For example, in stanza two, we had anticipated the indicative *contains,* not the subjunctive *contain* (perhaps the rime dictated the choice); in stanza one, the use of the participle *begun* for the indicative *began* does seem meaningful in suggesting that, so far as our memory is concerned, this pain had no beginning: it seems in retrospect always to have been *begun* before we remember its beginning. Thus at times the unusual syntactic forms do serve semantic purpose.

The meter is that of common measure, the first stanza scarcely riming (*recollect-not*), while the second has a perfect echo (*contain-pain*). The alliterative *p* sound of the second stanza stresses the word *pain,* focussing upon it as the central concern of the lines (*past-perceive-periods-pain*).

Of All the Souls That Stand Create (664)

Entitled "Choice" by its first editors (*Poems,* 1891), this lyric, like #303, reveals the poet's exclusiveness, her selection of one soul above all others. Here the selection is revealed in death, in eternity, when all shall see the soul's sovereign and irrevocable choice. Interestingly, the lyric focusses largely upon the images of death, sense and spirit separating, all pretense (subterfuge) ended, time ceased (that which is and that which was), the "shifting sands" of life ended, the "figures" (of God?) now seen face to face, the mist of the glass through which we see now cleared away. The theme of the lyric is conveyed in the first two and the last two lines essentially.

While the lyric is often printed as a single stanza, its meter and rime and arrangement (lines 5 and 9 starting anew with *when*) suggest it is actually three stanzas composed in common measure. Its rimes are perfect, again conveying a quality of sureness. There is a dominance of sibilant sounds which undercut the tranquillity however (*souls*-*s*tand-*sense*-*s*pirit-file*s*-*s*ubterfuge-i*s*-which-wa*s*-intrin*s*ic-*s*tand-thi*s*-fle*sh*-i*s*-*sh*ifted-*s*and-figure*s*-*s*how-mi*sts*-li*sts*). There are too a number of key words starting with the *f* sound (*f*iles-*f*lesh-*f*igures-*f*ront), showing Miss Dickinson's interest in phonetic echoes. (Note the unusual use of the word *create* where we had anticipated *created;* there are two instances of a similar use of the same form in Shakespeare, doubtless Miss Dickinson's source.)

Essential Oils Are Wrung (675)

All that is good and valuable in life is achieved through suffering. That is the theme of this brief lyric. Fragrant essences or perfumes are extracted under great pressures. Attar of roses (a fragrant oil pressed often from damask roses) is not alone the product of the sun, but of the screws of the press by which it is extracted as well. While roses generally blossom and die quickly, the attar of the rose retains its fragrant beauty, outlasting even the brevity of the lady's life who uses it (note the rosemary, a light blue flowering shrub, used both in cooking and as a perfume, is a symbol of remembrance and constancy).

The metric pattern is that of short meter, the rime dissonant in each case (*rose-screws;* in fact, the second stanza's rime, *drawer-rosemary,* is elusive and scarcely definable as rime). There is, too, as near a rime in lines 1 and 3 of each stanza (*wrung-alone, decay-lie*) as in lines 2 and 4. The alliteration of *s* sounds (*s*uns-*s*crews-*s*ummer-*c*easeless) is added to the play upon the rose (first as the perfume attar of roses; then the general garden rose and the echo in the rosemary).

A Thought Went Up My Mind Today (701)

Here Emily Dickinson describes that experience we all have had of a sudden thought, a flash of memory, a feeling that what we are now experiencing we have experienced before. She conveys perfectly the momentary pause and confusion such an experience gives us. The whole event is strange and imprecise; we can't quite remember when it was or where we had thought such a thing before. It eludes us as quickly as it came; yet we are certain we have met such a moment before.

The metric pattern is that of common measure, the first two rimes slant (*before-year, me-say*), the third perfect (*before-more*). The early bafflement is suggested in the imperfect rimes, the casual dismissal of the whole in the perfect concluding rime.

Publication Is the Auction (709)

Cited often as Emily Dickinson's reason for disdaining publication of her poems in her lifetime, the lyric does construct an elaborate argument against such merchandising of one's mind. Publication is so "foul," only the excuse of poverty could be forgiven in such a deed. What one has written is his very soul (his inmost thought), and the soul belongs to God (who gave it), and only secondarily to the body in which it is housed. To sell it (the royal air or breath which rules the body) is to make merchandise of the heavenly grace (God's gift); to put a price upon it in the marketplace is to disgrace the human spirit out of which thought rises.

While the metric pattern is basically common measure, it illustrates a number of variations, particularly Emily Dickinson's frequent habit of robbing a syllable from lines 2 and 4 of a stanza and placing it at the ends of lines 1 and 3. The effect is to give each line a strong (stressed) start and yet to allow lines 2 and 4 an equally strong ending.

```
    (x)/ x/   xx   x/   x,
    ⌣/   x/   x/
    (x)/ xx   x/   x/   x,
    ⌣/   x/   x/
  5 (x)/ xx   x/   x/   x,
    ⌣/   x/   x/
    (x)/ xx   x/   x/   x
    ⌣/   x/   x/

    (x)/ x/   x/   x/   x,
 10 ⌣/   x/   x/
    /x   /x   x/   x/   x,
    ⌣/   x/   x/

    (x)/ x/   x/   x/   x,
    ⌣/   x/   x?x/
 15 (x)/ x/   //   x/   x,
    ⌣/   x/   x/
```

Again we see her love of certain consonants used alliteratively (*p*ub-lication-*p*overty-*p*ossibly-*p*arcel-*p*rice—note also cor*p*oreal-s*p*irit; *m*ind-*m*an; *f*or-*f*oul; *b*elong-*b*ear-*b*e-*b*ut; *g*arret-*g*ave-*g*race—note also dis*g*race) and consonantally (*it*s-*ill*us*t*ra*t*ion-*s*e*ll*-*p*ar*c*e*l*-gra*c*e-redu*c*e-s*p*irit-*d*is*g*ra*c*e-*p*ri*c*e).

Because I Could Not Stop for Death (712)

Entitled "The Chariot" by its first editors (*Poems*, 1890), the lyric treats the subject of human death in an unusual way. The poet has died before writing the lyric. She looks back upon her own death (a situation asking Coleridge's "willing suspension of disbelief"). Writing from such a vantage does give the lyric greater "authority": an account of death by one who has died!

Death itself plays an unusual role: he is the driver of a carriage which houses only the poet and her escort, Immortality. The three of them ride about the countryside on a symbolic journey, passing the children at play (childhood), the ripened grain (maturity), the sunset (old age); we sense the chill of evening (death, the setting in of the rigor mortis); we see the party dress (of gossamer and tulle) which one might wear to an evening social event (but which here is worn as the body lies in the coffin) and "a house" like a swelling of the ground (the low mound of the grave). But Emily Dickinson does not stop there on her metaphorical journey with her courteous wooer; she takes us beyond the grave into eternity (the centuries passing in a word), and only there does the sudden realization come upon her: the horses which carried her through life face ultimately toward eternity where she finally awakens. That realization takes the sting out of death and causes the poet to contemplate it in a childlike way, dramatizing in her own mind the circumstances of the event.

The metric pattern is that of common measure (except that "The dews" of line 14 should appear in the previous tetrameter line). Except for the first stanza, the rimes are all imperfect, perhaps suggesting the slight contradiction between what is actually said and what our minds are thinking in the dramatization. There are numbers of examples of alliteration (*c*ould-*k*indly-*c*arriage in stanza one; *k*new-*n*o and *l*abor-*l*eisure in stanza two; *s*lowly-*c*ivility-*s*chool-*s*trove-*s*etting-*s*un in stanzas two and three; *r*ecess-*r*ing and *g*azing-*g*rain in stanza three; *d*ews-*d*rew, *g*ossamer-*g*own, and *t*ippet-*t*ulle in stanza four; *s*eemed-*s*welling-*s*carcely-*s*ince-*c*enturies-*s*urmised in stanzas five and six; *h*orses' *h*eads in stanza six; note too how *paused* in stanza five picks up phonetically the repeated *passed* in earlier stanzas), assonance (n*o*t-st*o*p-st*o*pped in stanza one; sl*o*wly-dr*o*ve-n*o* in stanza two; g*a*zing-gr*ai*n in stanza three; p*a*ssed-r*a*ther in stanzas three and four; d*ew*s-dr*ew* in stanza four), and consonance (be*c*ause-*c*ould-*c*arriage, *c*ould-*d*eath-*k*in*d*ly-stoppe*d*-he*ld*, bu*t*-jus*t*-immor*t*ality in stanza one; *s*carcely-*c*orni*c*e-*s*in*c*e in stanzas five and six, added to the alliterative *s* sound above; '*t*is-*c*en*t*uries-feel*s*-*s*urmi*s*ed-*h*or*s*es-*h*eads in stanza six).

Remorse Is Memory Awake (744)

Entitled "Remorse" by her first editors (*Poems*, 1891), the lyric is another of Emily Dickinson's definitions. The dictionary defines *remorse* as a deep sense of guilt which tortures one. Emily Dickinson elaborates that definition, giving it concreteness. Remorse is the continual presence of deeds done earlier, the inability of memory to escape them. It is the soul viewing its past in full and terrible light to the end that the soul be profited by such perusal. It is a "disease" which even God cannot cure, for it is of His doing, the earthly hell (it is a *sufficient* hell for any soul—a laconic understatement) to which He ordains human beings.

The metric pattern is that of common measure. The rimes are imperfect, ironically yoking *heal* and *hell* in the concluding stanza. There are intricate echoes of sounds, especially alliteration (*p*arties-*p*resence-*p*ast-*p*erusal, *d*eparted-*d*oor-*d*own-*d*isease, *s*et-*s*oul-*s*tretch, *h*eal-*h*is-*h*ell) and consonance (*r*emo*rs*e-*m*e*m*ory, he*r*-pa*r*ties-a*s*ti*r*-p*r*esence-*d*eparte*d*-*d*oor, remor*s*e-cureles*s*, i*s*-di*s*ease-ti*s*-hi*s*).

Renunciation Is a Piercing Virtue (745)

Like the preceding lyric, this is another of Miss Dickinson's definitions. *Renunciation* is defined by the dictionary as the formal and voluntary giving up of a right or claim, often at great sacrifice. Miss Dickinson begins with a similar abstract statement: renunciation is the letting go of something present for the hope of something future (the word takes on a religious connotation for her, the sacrificing of pleasure now for bliss in heaven).

Then she dramatizes. Renunciation is the putting out of one's eyes lest love of sight should compete with love of the Creator of sight (day). It is making a choice to one's own disadvantage because one has in view some greater good (a "larger function"); and, to return to the earlier image of sight, it is that greater good (the greater vision) which enables us to endure temporary blindness ("covered vision") here.

The metric of the lyric is irregular, especially in the arrangement of lines:

```
     x/   x/   xx   x/   x/x
     x/   x/                        go ⎤
     x/   xx   x/   x/x             now ⎦
     //
  5  x/   x/   x/                   eyes ⎤
     x/x                            sunrise ⎦
     //                             day ⎤
     //   x/   x/
     //.                            outvie ⎦
 10  x/   x/   xx   x/x
     x/   x/                        itself ⎤
     x/   x/   x/
     x/   x/                        itself ⎦
     x/   x/x
 15  //   x/                        appear ⎤
     /x   x/   x/   x/              here ⎦
```

It surely could not be argued that Emily Dickinson was insensitive to meter, guilty of want of control rhythmically. Too many of the lyrics of this same period give evidence of her skill. Instead, we must assume she has some purpose in the starts and stops (perhaps to convey the difficulty of and her reluctance in renouncing what is loved for some higher good). Alliteration (*p*iercing-*p*resence-*p*utting-*p*rogenitor, *v*irtue-*v*ision [though some would question two words so far from one another]) plays a small part in the lyric's beauty, along with unusual plays upon words (e. g., the repetition of *itself* in lines 11-13) and highly compressed utterance.

My Life Had Stood a Loaded Gun (754)

The lyric has fascinated many critics and general readers alike by its apparent allegorization of life. Yet all seem puzzled by the metaphorical meaning implicit in the allegorical figures. The life is compared to a loaded gun, taken by its master (God? Satan? evil?) to the woods where the doe is to be struck down. The gun is only an instrument in the "master's" hands, "speaking" for him (with the fiery flash and glow of the powder), lying protectively at his side, making his foe its foe (laying its "yellow eye" or "emphatic thumb" upon his enemies). But the concluding stanza is puzzling. It is obvious enough that a gun can outlast its mortal master (though, paradoxically, the master has an immortal soul which requires him to live after the gun is rusted and gone); yet strangely the gun-life is also immortal, having the power to kill-destroy, but not the power to die (in one sense, what is meant is perhaps that the gun has not actually been alive; thus it could not die, having no soul, no intangible being). The image shifts and is thrown perplexingly out of focus at the end (perhaps what is meant in the last line is only that the destructive work of the gun cannot end, its consequences continue).

The metric pattern is that of the common measure, only the first and last rimes perfect; all the others are appropriately dissonant, suggesting the troubled state of the lyric. There are examples of alliteration (*l*ife-*l*oaded and *c*orners-*c*arried in stanza one; *w*e-*w*oods, *s*overeign-*s*peak-*s*traight-*s*mile-*s*uch, and *v*alley-*V*esuvian in stanzas two and three; *d*ay-*d*uck's-*d*eep-*d*eadly in stanzas four and five; *l*onger-*l*ive-*l*onger in stanza six) and consonance (*st*ood-*l*oa*ded*-pa*ssed*-i*d*en-*tified*-carri*ed* in stanza one; roa*m*-ti*m*e-hi*m*-*m*ountains in stanza two; smi*l*e-cordia*l*-*l*ight-va*ll*ey-g*l*ow in stanza three; *d*ea*dly*-*lay*-ye*ll*ow in stanza five).

Presentiment Is That Long Shadow on the Lawn (764)

In this, another of her definition lyrics, Emily Dickinson concretizes the meaning of presentiment. The dictionary defines the term as a sense of foreboding, a premonition that something, especially something unhappy, is about to happen. Miss Dickinson describes it as a "long shadow," not the actuality, but the dark shadow which precedes night (the symbol of evil or misfortune). Presentiment is a notice served upon the grass, telling it that darkness is about to pass over it and consume it in its gloom.

The metric is unusual here, the first line a hexameter (suggesting the lengthening shadows), the last three tetrameters:

```
//  x/  x/  //  xx  x/
x/  x/  x/  //
x/  x/  x/  x/
x/  x/  x/  x/
```

The rime of the first couplet is imperfect (*lawn-down*), that of the second perfect (*grass-pass;* a circumstance which leads some to believe Emily Dickinson is describing in the second couplet a presentiment of a happy circumstance, the morning shadow's message to the grass is that darkness is about to pass on, to be replaced by day). Note the large number of sibilants (pre*s*entiment-i*s*-*s*hadow-*s*un*s*-notice-*s*tartled-gra*ss*-darkne*ss*-i*s*-pa*ss*) as well as other effects (the alliteration of *l*ong-*l*awn, the picking up of "go down" alliteratively in "grass" and "darkness").

The Hallowing of Pain (772)

The theme of this brief lyric is that before one can experience the hallowing of pain, the ritual meaning of it, he must have experienced it absolutely (a totality of pain whose end is surely death). Such a realization lies at the peak of the mountain of suffering (an unusual metaphor, since it suggests one must strive to know pain utterly) and is known only by those who reach that summit. If one wishes to comprehend that all-encompassing and sacred wisdom of pain, he must be willing to pay the supreme sacrifice of utter suffering.

The metric pattern here is that of short measure, the potential sing-song avoided by the slow tempo of the lines, the division of thought (the first three lines each require end pause) as contrasted with the run-on of certain passages (for example, line 4 runs into the second stanza, a thought which does not end until line 7; line 8 stands alone). While the rimes are imperfect, the first (*heaven-given*) suggests the hymnal in its common association of the two words. Emily Dickinson makes good use again of alliteration (*h*allowing-*h*eaven-*h*im-*wh*o-*h*ill-*h*e, *c*orporeal-*c*ost, *s*ummit-*s*trive*s*-*s*evere, *p*ain-*p*rice [some will argue against it, but in a number of lyrics, a strong consonant in an opening line is echoed in the last]).

The Birds Begun at Four O'Clock (783)

Emily Dickinson describes the early morning excitement of the birds, gathered in large numbers to start the day and then disappearing almost as suddenly. They have their own "dawn" (4 A.M.), their music filling up the space about them (note the odd use of "numerous" as a quantifiable modifier; we might say "numerous books," but not "numerous space"), as friendly ("neighboring") as noonday.

There was no identifying the individual voices in the music, any more than one could identify the brooks whose waters have composed the pond. There were no witnesses, except an occasional worker forced by his labor to get up before dawn, so surely they didn't sing for "applause." Their ecstasy did not depend upon either God or men; it was somehow wholly of themselves (note the inversion of "independent ecstasy"). As suddenly as it began, the music ceased (by 6 A.M.). Day came and the song of the birds is forgotten.

While the metric pattern of the first stanza is that of common measure, stanzas two through six are composed in short measure (note the elision of an accented syllable in line 19). The rimes are all dissonant (*dawn-noon, expend-pond, man-morn, ascertain-men, been-gone, world-fulfilled*), conveying the slight perplexity of the poet. There are numerous examples of phonetic repetition in the lines: alliteration (*b*irds-*b*egun, *f*our-*f*or-*f*orce, *n*umerous-*n*eighboring-*n*oon, *c*ould-*c*ount, *b*rook-*b*estows, *w*itnesses-*w*ere, *m*an-*m*orn, *d*one-*d*ressing-*d*eparture-*d*ay, *b*een-*b*and, *f*orgotten-*f*ulfilled), assonance (m*u*sic-n*u*merous, c*ou*ld-br*oo*k-br*oo*k, h*o*mely-*o*vertake-m*o*rn-n*o*r, independ*e*nt-*e*cstasy-m*e*n, fl*oo*d-d*o*ne), and consonance (numerou*s*-*s*pace, their-*f*orce-their, ex*p*end-multi*p*ly-*p*ond, wa*s*-applau*s*e, *as*certain-ec*s*ta*s*y, i*n*depe*n*de*n*t-me*n*, engro*ss*ed-ea*s*t, contro*ll*ed-wor*l*d-mirac*l*e- fu*l*-filled).

Bereaved of All I Went Abroad (784)

Entitled "Trying to Forget" by its earliest editors (*Poems,* 1896), the lyric suggests how difficult it is to escape one's own sense of loss and dramatizes the poet's fruitless efforts to escape. She pictures herself upon a journey whose goal is a recovery from the loss of one in death, upon some "new peninsula"—but the grave has arrived there before her (note the use of the grave as a metonymy for death). It lies upon her bed at night, follows her about in the day (note the unusual switch of phrases in lines 11-12: the more conventional form would be, "to *lose* it in the crowd, to *drop* it in the sea"), and even torments her rest (perhaps induced by a sedative, "artificial drowse"). While the dead are dead and that should end it, the "spade" remains in the memory. She cannot escape the bereavement of death, no matter how she struggles to.

The metric pattern is that of common measure, stanzas two and three containing perfect rimes, stanzas one and four dissonant rimes.

There are numerous examples of alliteration (*w*ent-*w*as, *p*eninsula-*p*receded-*p*illow, *f*ind-*f*irst-*f*ollowed, *s*ea-*s*teep-*s*pade), assonance (b*e*-r*ea*ved-pr*e*ceded-m*e*, w*a*ked-*a*w*a*ke, sh*a*pe-*a*w*a*y-gr*a*ve-sp*a*de-re-m*ai*ned), and consonance (be*r*eaved-ab*r*oad, *n*ew-pe*n*i*n*sula, re*p*osed-u*p*on-*p*illow, t*r*ied-*d*rop-c*r*ow*d*, lo*se*-drow*se*).

Ample Make This Bed (829)

In a letter, Emily Dickinson referred to this lyric as "Country Burial." In it, the poet orders her grave (bed) made "ample" and with sufficient awe to hold the corpse until it rises to the final judgment. She asks that it be buried deep enough, with mattress and pillow, that it will not be discovered by accident, not exposed to the sun's yellow "noise" (as though its rays of intense heat were virtually audible). While it appears composed in short measure, the lyric's lines start with accented syllables (the unaccented syllables elided), giving each line the emphasis of an awesome command:

```
  (x)/  x/  x/
  (x)/  x/  x/
  (x)/  x/  x/  x/
  (x)/  x/  x/
5 (x)/  x/  x/
  (x)/  x/  x/
  (x)/  x/  x/  x/
  (x)/  x/  x/
```

The pauses required by the elisions of course slow the tempo and provide an appropriate solemnity. Despite its brevity, the lyric is carefully wrought, the dominance of long *a* sounds at the first half (*make-wait-break-straight*) giving way to the diphthongs of the latter half (*round-noise-ground*). *Pillow* is heard again in *yellow*. The cacophony of the sibilants in the second stanza (*its-mattress-straight-its-sunrise'-noise-this*) all but void the perfect rime of *round-ground*.

There Is a Finished Feeling (856)

Here is another of those lyrics showing Emily Dickinson's fascination with death and the grave in the mid-1860's. This time she speaks of the sense of conclusion which one feels in facing loss in death. One senses a finality in death which changes life utterly by its vastness, virtually destroying our conviction of the future. Yet each experience of another's death enables us to examine more precisely our own lives, to understand more fully "what we are" and the function or purpose of the "eternal."

While the lyric is composed in common measure, the elisions of accented syllables at the ends of each of the tetrameter lines give an instance of hesitation (the missing stressed syllables are to be taken out in pause) which slows the tempo decidedly. The dissonant rimes (*graves-size, are-infer*) are appropriate to the gravity of intention. There are again the interests in phonetic repetition (the alliteration of *f*inished-*f*eeling-*f*uture-*f*unction, the echo of *leisure-future* and *exhibition-function,* the assonance of *is-finished*, the sibilance of i*s*-fini*s*hed-experien*c*ed-grave*s*-lei*s*ure-wilderne*ss*-*s*ize-death'*s*-e*x*hibition-pre*c*i*s*er, the consonance of *f*unction-in*f*er; note too the use of the capitalized *E* in *Experienced-Exhibition-Eternal-Enabled,* at least effective upon the eye in the reading).

(Note the adjectival form *preciser* in line 6 functioning as an adverb; is the fuller syntax: "We are enabled to infer in a preciser way what we are," or "We are enabled to infer more precisely what we are"?)

Split the Lark and You'll Find the Music (861)

Entitled "Loyalty" by its first editors (*Poems,* 1896), the lyric gives ironic advice to the skeptic who will not believe without sensory evidence. It is as foolish at times to seek such "proof" as it would be to carve the lark in search of the song he sings (as if you could find the pages of the score with bulblike notes upon them), a lovely song which is still welcome when the music of the lute is tiresome and stale.

It is a question whether she indeed speaks of a flood in stanza two, or simply uses it as the metaphor of the lark's "flood of song"; I believe the latter is the case, the image being that of the song pulled endlessly from the entrails of the lark. But such a bloody experiment can only fail and would, for that matter, be indulged only by a doubting Thomas (the allusion is to St. John XX, a passage in which the skeptical apostle refuses to believe Christ has risen unless he can thrust his finger into the wounds and his hand into the side).

Whether there is a larger meaning, some message on the subject of doubt and faith, of the scientific method as it challenges the instinctive trust of the believer, will depend upon the individual response to the lines.

The metric pattern is that of long measure, the accents ranging freely:

```
   /x   /x   x/   x/x
   /x   x/   x/   x/
   /x   x/   xx/  x/x
   /x   //   x/   x/
5  /x   /x   x/   x/x
   /x   x/   x/   x/
   /x   x/   xx/  x/x
   /x   x/   xx/  x/
```

(It is also possible in certain lines to see the pattern as anapestic with the unstressed syllables elided at the start of the lines; note, for example, line 8:

```
   [xx]/   xx/   xx/   [x]x/.)
```

Apparently Miss Dickinson means to reinforce the irony of the lines by the reliance on the cacophony of sibilants (*split-silver-scantily-summer-saved-shall-gush-gush-scarlet-experiment-sceptic-Thomas*). There are other phonetic effects as well: note the consonance of *split-lark-you'll-bulb-silver-rolled-scantily-delt* and *scarlet-experiment-sceptic-Thomas* and the catching of "bulb after bulb" in "gush after gush."

Till Death Is Narrow Loving (907)

The lyric contrasts mortal and eternal love, the finite love of human beings with the eternal love of immortal lovers. It catches the phrase from the marriage vows ("till death do us part") and argues that such love is scant indeed. The stingiest heart could vow such narrow, finite love (death is the moment when the "privilege of finiteness" is "spent").

But that love is far greater which, when his death ("loss") leaves you so destitute you can no longer live for your own sake, causes you to "imitate" him until you are utterly like him ("resemblance perfect") and finally makes you renounce natural being to follow him in death—that is love indeed (note how the "somewhat" gives a laconic quality of understatement to the passage).

Because much of the vocabulary suggests Biblical allusion, there are inevitable religious overtones. The lover calls to mind Christ, to whose perfect image the saint is to be conformed in eternity. Such a conviction creates in the child of God (His bride) an eagerness to "abdicate delight of nature" for His presence. Of course, these overtones are not central to the lyric's sense, but are meant to intensify the images of human love.

The metric pattern is that of common measure (though the first lines of each stanza are wanting in the final accented syllable). The rimes, while all imperfect, all conclude with the *t* sound (*extant-spent, that-imitate, pursuit-somewhat*). While this lyric does not contain so many examples of alliteration, assonance, and consonance as do others, it does illustrate Miss Dickinson's fondness for certain consonant sounds (*d, p, s*) appearing in positions of prominence (*d*eath-*d*estitution-*d*elight, *p*rivilege-*p*rocures-*p*erfect-*p*ursuit, *s*cantest-*s*pent-*s*uch-*s*omewhat; note also the consonantal use of them).

The Heart Has Narrow Banks (928)

Here Emily Dickinson describes the heart's potential turmoil chiefly in the metaphor of the sea. It flows on in steady measured cadence, its vastness nonetheless undisturbing to its calm. However, when the hurricane (some great emotional disturbance, some "storm" of life) comes, the sea's banks cannot contain it. No more can the heart, convulsed by some enormous trial, contain itself, but bursts its walls (as fragile as gauze) and rushes on uncontrolled. The slightest pressure "demolishes" the heart's walls, an inquisition "dissolves" it. (Note: this lyric was composed likely in 1864, as Emily Dickinson was recovering from the great emotional crisis of two years earlier.)

The metric pattern of the lyric is that of short measure. The rimes of the first two stanzas are perfect (*sea-monotony, discerns-learns*), that of the third imperfect (*gauze-dissolves*); the effect is to come with surprise (much as the "push" does to the heart) upon the slant echo.

The lyric is alive with phonetic effects: alliteration (*h*eart-*h*as-*h*urricane-*h*eart, *b*anks-*b*ass-*b*lue-*b*isect, *m*easures-*m*ighty-*m*onotony, *c*onvulsive-*c*alm-*q*uestioning, *d*iscerns-*d*emolishes-*d*issolves) being one of the chief organizing devices of sound. It is supported by both assonance (*itse*lf-*di*scern*s*-*its*-*in*suffi*c*ient) and consonance (note how the *m* sound of *unremitting* fits the *m*-alliterative pattern and how the sibilants are woven throughout the fabric [ha*s*-bank*s*-measure*s*-*sea*ba*ss*-bi*s*ect-a*s*-it*s*elf-di*s*cern*s*-it*s*-in*s*uffi*c*ient-convul*s*ive-learn*s*-i*s*-gauze-in*s*tant'*s*-pu*sh*-demoli*shes*-que*s*tioning-di*ss*olves]).

Unto Me? I Do Not Know You (964)

This dialogue between poet and Christ catches Him at the conclusion of His invitation "Come unto Me." The poet is at first alarmed because she neither knows Him nor where He dwells. His reassurance that He is Jesus, dwelling at present in Paradise, does not satisfy the poet. She wonders how she will arrive there (the pattern of the dialogue may be meant to suggest she is at the point of death) and is assured that His all-powerful arms will be her Phaeton (an allusion to the youth who drove Apollo's sun chariot across the sky—Emily Dickinson uses it only in the sense of the supernatural carriage).

Immediately the poet's mind leaps to the question of her own imperfectness and insignificance; but He is Pardon and the Giver of significance to those in His realm. At last the poet's questions are all resolved, and we assume she has given up her insecurity and doubt for the loving and all-sufficient Savior's wooing.

The metric pattern of the lyric is that of common measure (despite its rhythmic variants and divisions into two-line stanzas in some editions, the rime shows that the couplets are actually parts of quatrains):

```
      (x)/   x/   x/   x/   x
    / x/   x/
      (x)/   x/   xx/   x/   x
    / x/   x/
  5   (x)/   x/   xx   x/   x
    / x/   x/
      (x)/   x/   x/   x/x   x
    / x/   x/
      (x)/   x/   x/   x/   x
 10 / x/   x/
      xx   /x   /x   x/   x
    / x/   x/
```

The casting of the lyric in dialogue accounts for the implied pauses in elided syllables and often for its start of an apparently iambic line in a stressed syllable (it usually makes the utterance more commanding).

Death Is a Dialogue Between (976)

As in lyric 964, the poet here casts her meaning into the form of a succinct dialogue, this time between the Spirit and the Dust, but the whole performance is an effort to define death. Death commands the Spirit to dissolve, but the Spirit is not subject to death (it is immortal, entrusted by God to the temporary dwelling of the body, the Dust). Death gains his argument from the only source he knows, the "ground" (note the pun—the ground of his argument is the ground, the earth, the dust out of which the body is formed): he knows only mortality and cannot comprehend the immortal Spirit. The Spirit does not argue, but merely casts off its "overcoat of clay," the mortal flesh with which it had only temporarily dressed itself.

The metric pattern is that of common measure, the rimes perfect (perhaps to suggest the Spirit's invincible confidence). There is, especially in the first stanza, a predominance of d and s sounds alliteratively (death-dialogue-dust-dissolve-death-doubts, spirit-says-spirit-sir-spirit), supported by the large number of t sounds and sibilants (between-spirit-dust-spirit-trust-doubts-it-spirit-turns-overcoat, is-dust dissolve-says-trust-doubts-argues-turns-just-evidence).

A Narrow Fellow in the Grass (986)

Entitled "The Snake" when published anonymously in the *Springfield Daily Republican* (February 14, 1866), the lyric is one of several descriptive of "nature's people" (note 1356, 1575, 1463, and others). It starts with a seemingly objective account. The serpent "rides" along in the grass (a remarkable preciseness: the snake does not walk or crawl, but simply glides along). He doesn't give much notice of his arrival; we see only the grass parting and closing as his "spotted shaft" moves along.

Samuel Bowles, the editor of the *Springfield Daily Republican* commented upon his own surprise that a girl would know that corn won't grow in a boggy field. Yet Emily Dickinson not only knows that, she plays the role of a lad, playing barefoot at noon, spying the snake (mistaking it for a whiplash), reaching for it as it rides elusively on ("wrinkled" is again the perfect word).

The lyric ends with the poet speaking of her hostility toward the creature, how he sends the chill upon her and makes her breathe more heavily. Some critics have interpreted that hostility (and the whole of the poem's contents) as suggesting Miss Dickinson's apprehension about sex. They see her New England spinsterhood as the necessary result of her emotional frigidity.

The metric pattern is that of common measure (though final accented syllables are elided from lines 9, 11, 13, 15, 17, 19, 21, 23). The rimes of the first four stanzas are slant (*rides-is, seen-on, corn-noon, sun-gone*), those of the final two stanzas are perfect (*me-cordiality, alone-bone*). The phonetic organization of this lyric is not so tight as that of others, but examples of alliteration (*may-met* and *not-notice* in stanza one; *spotted-seen* and *feet-further* in stanza two; *cool-corn* and *boggy-boy-barefoot* in stanza three; *sun-stooping-se-cure-several* and *nature's-know-never* in stanzas four through six; *but-breathing-bone* in stanza six), assonance (*floor-corn* and *too-cool-noon* in stanza three; *have-passed-lash* in stanza four; *never-met-fel-low-attended* in stanza six), and consonance (*fellow-occasionally* and *narrow-grass-rides* in stanza one; *passed-whip-stooping-people* in stanzas four and five) do appear.

Crumbling Is Not an Instant's Act (997)

The theme of this lyric is stated in the first line: when a man or an institution falls into ruin, you can know that there is behind the crash a slow and steady process of decay. The whole is cast into the metaphor of a building's collapse: the cobwebs, the dust, the eating away of the structure which holds the building up—all is a slow, but persistent progress toward ruin. No man ever fell "in an instant"; he slipped and slipped until the crash finally destroyed him.

The metric pattern is that of common measure (an accented syllable elided at the end of line 7), the first and third rimes slant (*pause-decays, slow-law*), the second perfect (*dust-rust*). Here again can be observed Emily Dickinson's giving dominance to certain consonant sounds alliteratively as an organizing principle (*crumbling-cob-web-cuticle-consecutive-crash's, pause-processes, dilapidation's-de-cays-dust-devil's*).

Blind Me—I Still Can Sing (1005)

This is essentially a love lyric, the soul's protest that it can delight in love even when the body is abused. If bound, the soul can still sing (note the ambiguity of line two: "Banish [me], my mandolin / Strikes true within" or "Banish my mandolin, [it] / Strikes true within"). Even if slain, the soul can sing its way to paradise, still confident that she is her lover's.

The metric form is not clearly established, the lines not elaborately organized:

```
    //   x/  x/
    /x   x/  x/
    //   x/
    /x   x/  x/
 5  /x   x/  x/
    //
```

Nonetheless, it is clear that the shorter third line in each case gives a note of surprise, a quality of determination to the whole. Despite its brevity, the lyric does show the poet's phonetic interests, especially in alliteration (*b*ind-*b*anish, *s*till-*s*ing-*s*trikes-*s*lay-*s*oul-*s*till, *m*e-*m*y-*m*an-dolin).

I Never Saw a Moor (1052)

One of her simplest lyrics, these lines convey a childlike faith in God, a certainty of reliance upon Him. The two stanzas are the metaphor and reality consecutively. While reared inland and never having seen sea or moor, the poet still knows what heather and billow are. By the same token, she is as certain of the spot where heaven stands (though she has never visited there) as if she were now on the train headed there, her checks (receipts for the ticket purchase) already in the conductor's hands.

The lyric is in short measure, a meter peculiarly appropriate to the child's utterance, containing just a hint of the sing-song of the imperfectly wrought rime. Despite the lyric's brevity, there are evidences of care in construction. The phonetic echoes of alliteration play an important part in the lines (*s*aw-*s*ea-*s*poke-*c*ertain-*s*pot, *n*ever-*k*now-*n*ever-*n*or, *h*ow-*h*eather-*h*eaven, *G*od-*g*iven).

Further in Summer Than the Birds (1068)

In a letter to Thomas Miles (March 1883), Emily Dickinson alluded to this lyric with the title "My Cricket." The language of the lines is abstruse, puzzling and dividing critics who have struggled with its meanings. The opening seems to suggest that the cricket remains long after the birds have taken their flight, that the pathetic song of the insignificant creature (a "minor nation" suggesting both the creature's unimportance and the sad, minor quality of its song) can be heard in the grass. The cricket's celebration (its mass) cannot be seen; only its voice is heard (note how many of the words take on a religious connotation: *celebrates-Mass-ordinance-gradual-grace-canticle*). But the response of the listener is distinct: it is one of loneliness, creating "spectral" images in the hot August sun. Yet to the humble creature there is remitted as yet no grace (he has no part in redemption; it may not exaggerate the symbols here to see some identification on the poet's part between her own plight and the cricket's; she has had no remission of grace either). The cricket's song, while it appears while summer yet retains its glow, gives to nature a Druidic quality (something akin to the mysterious ceremonies of the ancient Celtic worshippers).

As she often does, Miss Dickinson mixes metric patterns, constructing stanza one after the common measure, stanza two through four after the short measure; the chief effect is to broaden the opening line (the one point of difference in the two patterns) and give it greater prominence. The rimes, after those of stanza one (*grass-Mass*), are imperfect (*grace-loneliness, low-typify, glow-now*), aiding the effect of gloom and loneliness which dominates the lyric.

Again we see the poet's absorbing interest in phonetic repetitions: the alliterations (*m*inor-*m*ass, *g*rass-*g*radual-*g*race-*g*race-*g*low, *l*oneliness-*l*ow, *r*epose-*r*emit, *D*ruidic-*d*ifference, *n*ation-*n*o-*n*oon-*n*o-*n*ature-*n*ow, *p*athetic-*p*ensive) are only a part of the total interest; consonance (fu*r*the*r*-su*mm*e*r*-bi*r*ds-g*r*a*ss*-*m*ino*r*, etc., g*r*adua*l*-g*r*ace-en*l*a*r*g-ing-*l*one*l*iness, *s*pe*c*tra*l*-*c*anti*cl*e-etc.) and assonance (n*a*tion-celebr*a*tes, c*u*stom-bec*o*mes) are also vital.

Title Divine Is Mine (1072)

Here appears another of those lyrics in which Emily Dickinson imagines herself as having experienced the fulfillment of marriage, as being now "wife" though without the outward trappings of a wedding (it was written in the year of Wadsworth's departure for California). There are yet a number of mysteries in the lyric: why, for example, does the poet refer to herself as "Empress of Calvary," unless she means to encapsulate her suffering in that image? (The use of religious words tempts us to think of the heavenly bride, the church, redeemed at Calvary; "born, bridalled, shrouded" could suggest conversion, which is spoken of as a new birth, as a betrothal to the Savior, and as a symbolic death; yet Wadsworth was a clergyman, and the imagery in those words may be conjured only in deference to him. Perhaps the concluding line is meant to ask: Is this way that I feel in spiritual marriage like what you women feel who have known earthly marriage?)

The meter is among the most irregular examples in the Dickinson lyrics. The first four lines appear in short measure (except that the rime is *aabb*), but lines 5-6 seem a trimeter couplet, lines 7-9 a badly-lined tetrameter couplet. And, while lines 11, 13, and 15 rime (and lines 12 and 14 appear to as well), it looks as though we have a three-line grouping, the first a trimeter line, the second and third pentameter lines. Far from detracting, the variations help to convey the exhilarated, if covertly distraught, state of mind.

1	/x	x/	x/			mine
2	x/	x/	x/			sign
3	x/	x/	x/	x/		me
4	/x	x/	x/			Calvary
5	/x	/x	x/			crown
6	x/	x/	x/			swoon
7	//	x/	x			
8				/	x/	hold
9	/x	x/	x	/	x/	gold
10	//	x/	x			
11				/	x/	day
12	//	xx				(victory)
13			//	x/	x/	say
14	/x	x/	xx			(melody)
15				x/	x/	way

The Bustle in a House (1078)

Another of her poems upon the theme of death, this brief lyric describes the response of the living to the death of one held dear, especially that response the "morning after death." There are always so many things to be done, particularly in a house where the wake will be held, setting all in readiness for the parade of relatives and friends who wish to "review the remains." Of course, it may be that, in Miss Dickinson's use of the word *death* she means to include burial as well. Her lyric suggests she is really describing that first lonely morning when the beloved dead must be put out of our thoughts to enable us to return to our normal lives. We must put love away until eternity when living and dead are reunited.

The metric pattern of both stanzas is that of short measure. There is not the complexity of phonetic pattern as in other of the lyrics, but a stillness, a simplicity of statement suitable to the quiet motion in a house just beseiged by death.

Revolution Is the Pod (1082)

Emily Dickinson here comments on the cyclic necessity of revolution. Out of revolution is born the new system, as the seed comes from the pod. It grows into a lovely flower. But unless the process is repeated every summer, the flower will only shrivel on the stalk. So revolution must succeed revolution, reviving the "systems" of our lives, or else the death of decay will consume them. Liberty, if it is to be kept alive, must live in a continual process of revolution and new birth, testing the older systems to see if they are still alive.

The stanzaic pattern is that of common measure; the rimes of stanzas two and three are perfect, that of stanza one imperfect. There is a complex pattern of alliteration (*r*evolution-*r*attle-*r*usset-*r*evolution, *s*ystems-*s*tirred-*s*ummer-*s*o-*s*talk, *p*od-*p*urple, *w*inds-*w*ill, *b*loom-*b*ut-*b*ase-*b*e, *l*iberty-*l*eft), as well as examples of assonance (*excellent*-*except*, fl*ed*-r*e*volution-t*e*st-d*ea*d, st*a*lk-*a*ll) and consonance (except-russet, its-russet-base, summer-entomber, liberty-left-inactive-stalk, purple-fled).

At Half-Past Three, A Single Bird (1084)

Chiefly here Emily Dickinson is intent upon conveying the exciting sound of the birds at song, at first a single bird, then a mighty voice which could be heard above all else. But as quickly as they came, they disappeared until, at seven-thirty, not one could be seen or heard: they were gone.

The primary organizing device is the passage of time, the first sound heard "at half-past three," the full chorus "at half-past four," and silence "at half-past seven." The start of the initial bird is cautious, shy, remote, but within an hour the "silver" music of their song dominates all else. Yet, by sunrise, the place from which they sang is empty, nothing of their earlier presence can be seen.

The metric pattern is that of common measure, each stanza starting a new phase of the experience. The rimes are perfect except in the first stanza (though it too is a common "eye-rime"). The phonetic fabric is wrought with intricate interchanges of alliterative (*single*-*silent*-*sky*-*single*-*subjugated*-*silver*-*supplanted*-*seven*-*seen*-*circum*-ference, *term*-*test*, *propounded*-*principle*-*place*-*presence*), assonantal (h*a*lf-p*a*st, s*i*lent-sk*y*, s*e*ven-*e*lement, b*e*-s*ee*n), and consonantal (pas*t*-*t*es*t*-p*r*inciple-*r*est, *element*-*implement*, pla*c*e-p*r*esen*c*e-*c*i*rc*umferen*c*e) patterns.

The Last Night That She Lived (1100)

In May of 1866, a Miss Laura Dickey had died while visiting her parents in Amherst. That incident is thought by some to have provoked Emily Dickinson's account here. Nothing was unusual about the evening of her demise, but her dying somehow altered even the commonest experiences. What may have appeared insignificant in any other light was "italicized" by the fact of death. The quiet motion back and forth between the rooms which housed the living and that which housed the dying underscored in a mysterious way the "jealousy" which the poet felt for the dying woman's life, as contrasted with the easy vitality of the living.

The moment of death itself "jostled" the soul, leaving it to stand silently and helplessly by, while the dying woman tried to speak (mentioned) but could not (forgot), struggled an instant before yielding to death (the simile of the frail reed swept into motion by the rushing water is a telling figure). Death accomplished, the living prepare the body for the long wake (the "awful leisure" when faith, shaken by the proximity of death, can be restored, regulated as it were).

The lyric is composed in short measure, the risks of sing-song overcome by the slower, heavily stressed lines (e. g., line 1: x/ /x //; line 4: // x/ x/; line 7: x/ // x/ x/; line 9: x/ // x/; line 10: x/ // x/; etc.) and the clusters of consonants which retard the tempo (e. g., line 1: *last night*; line 5: *We noticed smallest*

things; line 23: *struggled scarce*). The rimes are consistently dissonant, jarring expectation by the disappointment of their imperfection
(*night-different, before-'twere, room-blame, quite-infinite, time-
came, reed-dead, erect-regulate*). Examples of alliteration (*last-lived*
and *night-night-nature-noticed* in stanzas one and two; *before-by-be-
tween-blame* in stanzas two and three; *narrow-notice* and *souls-speak*
in stanza five; *struggled-scarce* in stanza six; *hair-head* in stanza
seven), assonance (*night-night-dying* and *made-nature* in stanza one;
light-minds-italicized in stanza two; *mentioned-bent-consented-dead*
in stanza six), and consonance (*last-night-that-it-night-except* in
stanza one; *her-room-rooms-where-tomorrow-were* in stanza three;
leisure-belief-regulate in stanza seven), as well as the use of sibilants
(*noticed-smallest-things-things-this-minds-italicized-as* in stanza two;
she-passed-was-jostled-souls-speak-notice in stanza five), greatly en-
hance the music of the lines.

After a Hundred Years (1147)

Entitled "The Forgotten Grave" when first published (*Poems,*
1891), the lyric may allude to the graves of soldiers who had died
earlier in the Civil War (it was written about 1869). Its theme is now
a commonplace of literature: as the years pass, men forget the soil
on which the great events of history were enacted (in fact, they forget the events themselves—or at least they forget their real implication). The "agony" of those momentous deeds can no longer be
discerned in the "motionless" peace of the landscape. (Note the unusual active form *enacted* in line 3, where we had anticipated the passive *was enacted*. It is as though the agony itself were personified and
acting out its role—no specific event enacted, but another "agony"
at work.)

Weeds overrun the monuments that had once marked the graves of
heroes. Only "strangers" (tourists and curiosity seekers, alien to the
incidents of a previous century) wander about the graveyard, struggling to read the unfamiliar names of the dead, the erosion of time
leaving the words scarcely discernible. Only the wind knows the spot,
remembering from summer to summer where those heroes lie.

The lyric is composed in short measure, considerable liberty taken
within the pattern:

```
/x   x/   x/
/x   x/   x/
```

```
   /x  x/  x/  x/
   (x)/  x/  x/

5  (x)/  x/  x/
   (x)/  x/  x/
   (x)/  x/  x/  x/
   (x)/  x/  x/

   (x)/  x/  x/
10 (x)/  x/  x/
   (x)/  x/  x/  x/
   (x)/  x/  x/
```

The repeated loss of opening unaccented syllables creates a stronger start for the lines, each after the third beginning with a stressed syllable; in addition, the lyric moves more slowly, the lost syllable taken out in pause. The rimes are all imperfect (*place-peace, spelled-dead, way-memory*), again supporting the disappointment in the tone throughout. There are here also interesting echoes of sound: the assonance of n*o*body-kn*o*ws-m*o*tionless, *a*gony-en*a*cted, and p*ea*ce-w*ee*ds; the consonance of *r*anged-*str*angers-*str*olled-*sp*elled and in*st*in*ct*-*p*i*ck*ing-u*p*-*k*ey-dro*pp*ed; the echo of *weeds* in *winds* accomplished by putting each in an initial position in the stanza and repeating consonant sounds (note too how the long *e* and *ds* sounds are heard in *fields*).

We Never Know How High We Are (1176)

Entitled "Aspiration" when first published (*Poems*, 1896), the lyric utters a familiar theme: when a man is called on in crisis to do something extraordinary, something perhaps he thought he could not do, he surprises himself and does it. When asked to rise above his "normal" abilities, a man stretches so tall he can touch the sky. Actually, the heroism we read about in books and recite proudly of the great men of the past would not seem so unusual, would in fact appear only "normal," were it not for our instinctive tendency to dwarf ourselves, to cut the cubits from our potential height, almost fearing we may indeed rise to some great endeavor (become a "king" among men).

The metric pattern is that of common measure, the rimes perfect (*rise-skies, thing-king*). Despite its brevity, its lyric succinctness, the poem relies heavily upon phonetic repetition for its effect; note particularly the alliteration of *never-kn*ow, *how-high-h*eroism, *true-t*ouch, *s*tatures-*s*kies, *we-w*ould-*w*arp, *n*ormal-*n*ot, *c*ubits-*k*ing, *for-f*ear.

He Preached upon "Breadth"
Till It Argued Him Narrow (1207)

Entitled "The Preacher" by its first editors (*Poems,* 1891), the lyric satirizes the exaggerations of an unknown clergyman who speaks with such self-confidence and easy volubility that his pretensions contradict the simplicity of the Biblical texts upon which his sermons are founded. "Breadth" and "Truth" are his subjects, but his garrulity reveals his own narrowness and dishonesty. Set alongside the humble and "innocent Jesus," his flauntings are obviously counterfeit. The poet cannot admire him (note the simile of gold and pyrites, the precious metal symbolizing the true qualities of which he speaks, the pyrites the falsity of the man's person).

The meter reminds us of common measure, except that it contains so many anapests and a number of unusual concluding feet (xx/x). These oddities create a clumsiness in recitation, the anapests giving a strange jog to the rhythm (perhaps to confirm the hypocrisy of the sense).

```
    x/   xx/   xx/   xx/x
    x/   xx/   xx/
    xx/   x/   xx/   xx/x
    x/   xx/   xx/

5   x/   xx/   xx/   xx/x
    x/   x/   xx/
    xx/   xx/   xx/      xx/x
    x/   xx/   xx/
```

The semantic organization is simple, each pair of lines built upon a contrast, upon an irony (*breadth-narrow, truth-liar, simplicity-counterfeit, gold-pyrites, Jesus-man*). The rime of the first stanza is perfect (*define-sign*) that of the second imperfect (*shun-man*). While the lyric relies primarily on the compressed and ironical statement of ideas, there are some alliterative effects (*p*reached-*p*roclaimed-*p*resence-*p*yrites, *s*ign-*s*implicity, *fl*aunted-*fl*ed, *c*ounterfeit-*c*onfusion-*c*over, *m*eet-*m*an).

A Word Dropped Careless on a Page (1261)

The power of the written word—that is the theme of this lyric. The author may drop a word upon the page with very little care; yet that word may have a great effect on some reader long after he is dead, "folded in perpetual seam." If the word is destructive, it may, like some contagious disease, breed despair in the reader centuries after it is written.

The metric pattern is common measure, the rime of the first stanza perfect (*eye-lie*) and that of the second imperfect (*despair-malaria* may be closer than is at first obvious, considering the New England habit of pronouncing the latter word with an added *r* sound). There are a number of unusual phonetic effects. Note especially how the consonants of the first, fourth, fifth, and seventh lines slow them down, requiring the reader to assimilate the meanings more carefully. Alliteration (*page-perpetual, seam-sentence-centuries, word-wrinkled, may-maker-may-malaria, despair-distances*), consonance (*word-dropped-folded-wrinkled, infection-in-inhale, distances-centuries*), and assonance (*page-may-maker-may-inhale*) play important roles as well.

There Is No Frigate Like a Book (1263)

Entitled "A Book" when first published (*Poems,* 1896), the lyric is one of Emily Dickinson's best known. Its theme is the pleasures which one may enjoy, the adventures made possible in the pages of an exhilarating book. Reading affords the excitement of travel, the exotic pageantry suggested in the parade of prancing horses. Its excitements are available to the poorest reader, asking no toll or charge of any. The lyric is enlivened by the sharp, precise images by which its meanings are conveyed: that of ship, of prancing coursers, of toll road and chariot, the human soul borne on its extravagant journey in the wonder of language.

The stanzaic pattern is common measure, the rime of the first stanza imperfect (*away-poetry*), that of the second perfect (*toll-soul*). There are a number of examples of alliteration (*like-lands-like, page-prancing-poetry-poorest, traverse-take-toll;* even *frigate-frugal* and *book-bears* echo one another within the compass of so brief a lyric), assonance (*take-away-page-may-take*), and consonance (*like-book-take-coursers, this-traverse-poorest-oppress, toll-frugal-soul*).

The Rat Is the Concisest Tenant (1356)

Entitled "The Rat" when first published in *Poems* (1891), the lyric is another of those about "nature's people," this time about the life and habits of the lowly rodent. He is a "concise" tenant (an unusual word here, suggesting the smallness, the compactness both of his size and of the housing he requires) who accepts no obligation to pay his share of rent. Try as we will, we can neither catch him nor escape his "schemes." No matter how we hate him, he is impervious to our designs on him. He knows no obligation to law, but is a law unto himself. There is a charm in Miss Dickinson's portrait of him, leaving the impression of her feeling of "cordiality" toward the creature.

The metric pattern is unusual (perhaps to suggest the same recalcitrance and resistance in the meter which is in the obstreperous nature of the rat). The quatrain contains a perfect rime (*rent-intent*) which is repeated in lines 2 and 4 of the sestet (*circumvent-reticent*); the two closing lines of the lyric rime imperfectly however (*him-equilibrium*).

```
    x/   x/   x/   x/x
    x/   //
    x/   x/   x/   x/x
    x/   x/

5   /x   x/
    x/   x/   x/
    //   x/
    x/   x/   x/
    /x   x/   x/   x/
    /x   x/   x/   x/
```

There are instances of alliteration (*rat-rent-repudiates-reticent, schemes-sound-circumvent, hate-harm-him*) and consonance (*rat-tenant-rent-intent-wit*, etc., *schemes-harm-him-equilibrium*).

A Route of Evanescence (1463)

In a letter to Higginson (November 1880), Emily Dickinson referred to this lyric as "A Humming-Bird." It is intended to describe this smallest of birds as it hovers in flight, its body lovely in the sun, its path one continual process of vanishing (we catch it in flight only as it evades our probing eyes), like an ever-revolving wheel of motion and color. It is not emerald itself, but "a resonance of emerald," like the green reflected radiance of that gem; it is a rush of crimson (like the cochineal, an insect used for making red colors). As it flits from flower to flower, the very blossoms are stricken by its beauty. So awesomely swift is it in its flight it could go to and return from Tunis in a morning. (This lyric makes an interesting comparison with #500. There is a fuller discussion in *Explicator*, VIII, 1950, Item 54.)

Though printed without a stanza break, the lyric is actually composed in common measure (a final accented syllable elided at the end of line 1). The first rime is perfect (*wheel-cochineal*), the second imperfect (*head-ride*). Though brief, the poem makes good use of alliteration(*r*oute-*r*evolving-*r*esonance-*r*ush-*r*ide, *b*lossom-*b*ush, *t*umbled-*T*unis, *m*ail-*m*orning's) and consonance (e*v*anescence-re*v*ol*v*ing, tumble*d*-hea*d*-ri*d*e).

How Happy Is the Little Stone (1510)

Called "Simplicity" by its first editors (*Poems,* 1891), the lyric praises the simple, mindless joy of the little stone in the road. He doesn't have to worry about a career (as we human beings do) or emergencies. He lies unworried as the universe moves along, not caring whether the sun shines or not, whether it is day or night. He fulfills without anxiety the role decreed for him—"casual simplicity." Of course, much of the force of the lyric comes from what it does not say—from the obvious contrast hinted at between the stone and the poet: all that she envies in it implies the complexity and trial of her own life.

The stanzaic pattern is that of the iambic tetrameter couplet, the free motion of the lines spurred on by the vitality and frequency of the rimes (all but two perfect: *stone-alone, careers-fears, decree-simplicity;* the four nasal rimes, while imperfect, hinder the lines but slightly: *brown-on-sun-alone*). Even in so carefree an evocation, Emily Dickinson interlaces the intricate effects of alliteration (*h*ow-*h*appy rambles-*r*oad, *c*are-*c*areers-*c*oat-*c*asual, *p*assing-*p*ut, *s*tone-*s*un-*s*implicity), assonance (st*o*ne-r*o*ad-al*o*ne, el*e*mental-ind*e*p*e*nd*e*nt, ass*o*ciates-gl*o*ws-al*o*ne), and consonance (pa*ss*ing-univer*s*e-a*ss*ociate*s*-ab*s*olute-*s*implicity).

As Imperceptibly as Grief (1540)

A poignant lyric of the passing of summer, this poem catches deftly at the figures of grief, of perfidy (by contrast), of stillness and withdrawal, the morning as a strange guest eager to be gone (perhaps *morning* is a metonymy for the sun whose growing shortness of duration as the summer passes is central in the figure), the fleet images of bird or whip escaping quickly into the "beautiful" (is the beauty of autumn with ripened fruit and grain and radiant leaves meant?). The poet emphasizes the quality of imperceptibility in the whole process; one scarcely notices the passage of summer until in final awareness it has gone.

Appropriate to the quiet grief which enshrouds the loss of summer's radiance are the intricate patterns of sibilance, both in alliteration and consonance (a*s*-imper*c*eptibility-a*s*-*s*ummer-lap*s*ed-inpercepti-ble-la*s*t-*s*eem-quietne*ss*-di*s*tilled-a*s*-*s*pending-her*s*elf-*s*eque*s*tered-du*s*k-*s*hone-courteou*s*-grace-a*s*-gue*s*t-thu*s*-*s*ervice-*s*ummer-e *s* c a p e). The effect is undergirded by other consonantal repetitions (e. g., the *p* sounds of *imperceptibly-lapsed* are caught up in the stronger *perfidy;* the *l* sounds of *imperceptibly-imperceptible-distilled-twilight-herself* are enforced by the alliterative *lapsed-last-like-long-light*). Note too the alliteration of *grace-guest-gone, drew-dusk, without-wing*. There are also striking assonantal repetitions (*lapsed-at-last, quietness-twilight, morning-foreign, made-escape*).

Despite its arrangement as a single stanza, the quatrain is clearly implied in the rime scheme (though all the rimes are imperfect: *away-perfidy, begun-afternoon, shone-gone, keel-beautiful*), as well as in the metric patterns borrowed from the hymnal (note that the first four lines are in common measure, the last twelve in three short-measure stanzas).

The Bible Is an Antique Volume (1545)

Emily Dickinson wrote this lyric for her nephew Ned who, because of illness, was unable to attend his college classes at Amherst (the reference is to the daily chapel which he was compelled to miss). Her attitude toward the Bible as here expressed has a touch of scorn or at least distrust in it (although the Bible and Shakespeare were her two prime sources of poetic inspiration). The Bible is archaic, she suggests, written by men now lost in the past (she alludes to the doctrine of inspiration by the Holy Spirit and to the visionary nature of such books as Ezekiel, Daniel, and the Revelation).

After listing some of its subjects—Bethlehem, Eden, Satan, David, sin—she contrasts the sober message of the Bible with that of the ancient Orpheus who, when he played his lute and sang, attracted even the trees of the forest to lean toward him to hear his captivating music. The Bible, in contrast, "condemns," requiring its hearers to walk a narrow, lonely way to be saved.

Here is hinted an attitude which the poet expresses elsewhere, both in other lyrics and in her letters, that if the love and graciousness of God were made real to men, none could resist Him.

The metric pattern is irregular, though it falls generally into four-line units (reminiscent of common measure, but free in accentual pattern):

```
     x/   x/   x/   x/x
     /x   x/   x/
     x/   x/   xx/  x/x
     (x)/  x/   x/
 5   /x   x/   x/x
     /x   x/   x/
     /x   x/   x/x
     /x   x/   x/
     /x   x/   x/   x/
10   (x)/  x/   x/
     /x   x/   x/   x/x
     (x)/  x/   x/
     x/   x/   x/   x/x
     (x)/  x/   x/
15   /x   x/   x/   x/x
     (x)/  x/   x/
```

The rimes are all dissonant (*men-Bethlehem, brigadier-troubador, resist-lost, come-condemn*), supporting the hint of unorthodoxy in the view expressed. The meaning is stated elementally, perhaps in deference to her twenty-one-year-old nephew to whom it was sent. There are instances of alliteration (*Bible-Bethlehem-brigadier-boys-believe-boys-boys, spectres-subjects-Satan-sin-sermon, holy-homestead, defaulter-David, lonesome-lost, tale-teller, captivated-condemn*), consonance (*Eden-ancient-Satan, brigadier-great-defaulter-David-troubador, distinguished-must-resist-lost, sermon-condemn*), and assonance (*Satan-great-David, sin-distinguished-precipice-resist, others-must*).

The Bat Is Dun with Wrinkled Wings (1575)

Entitled "The Bat" when it first appeared (*Poems,* 1896), the lyric is like several others in its description of one of "nature's people" (note also numbers 986, 1356, and 1463). The bat is dun in color (a dark, gloomy black or brown), fallow (perhaps used in the sense of a faded reddish color). Its wings are "wrinkled" as it stands (a precise visual evocation) and like half an umbrella as it glides through the air. It has no perceptible song (as other "birds" do), but describes an arc in its flight. (It is uncertain whether or not the poet means the bat's arc is as difficult to understand or see clearly as is the lofty, elate, proud philosopher's speculations: I suspect that is her point— particularly in the night can it not be clearly discerned. At any rate, the language of the passage is inflated and has about it something akin to the philosopher's jargon.)

We cannot guess from what "firmament" it has been sent, or where its shrewd dwelling is, or just what evil it may portend. Yet we must praise its Creator (God), whose very eccentricities (as delighting in such odd creations as bat and rat and snake) are meant for our good.

The stanzaic pattern is common measure (note the final accented syllables elided in stanza four), the rimes (all but the first odd instance—*article-perceptible*) are dissonant (*air-philosopher, abode-withheld, praise-eccentricities*), supporting the mild bewilderment occasioned by contemplation of this strange creation. There are instances of alliteration (*p*ervade-*p*erceptible, *f*allow-*ph*ilosopher-*f*rom-*f*irmament, *b*eneficent-*b*elieve), assonance (dep*u*ted-ast*u*te, with-mal*i*gnity-ausp*i*ciously-w*i*thheld, b*e*n*e*ficent-*e*cc*e*ntricities; note too the number of words starting with the capital A, doubtless an effect important to the eye: *A*rticle-*A*ir-*A*rc-*A*stute-*A*bode-*A*uspiciously), and consonance (*like* - *fallow* - *article* - *lips* - *perceptible* - *small* - *umbrella* - quain*tly*, ai*r*-a*rc*, wha*t*-firmamen*t*-wha*t*-as*tu*te, abo*d*e-empowere*d*-wi*th*hel*d*, a*d*roi*t*-crea*t*or).

Apparently with No Surprise (1624)

Entitled "Death and Life" by its first editors (*Poems,* 1890), the lyric is temptingly symbolic in its evocation. Ostensibly it is the record of the flower's death at the frost's guillotine. There is no surprise nor any great show of pomp at the event—the "blond assassin" (the frost) beheads its victim and moves along, as the sun indifferently marks off another day. God, like the God of Creation, sees all and declares it good. As I suggested earlier, we are tempted to see the account as symbolic of human life and death, the fragility of our beings, cut off by the sure hand of death, while the days pass and God looks approvingly on. (Whether or not there is intended, as some suggest, any irony in the last three lines, is a question not easily resolved. The poet may simply be asserting that this is all as God had purposed it, and so He "approves" its accomplishment.)

While the lyric is often printed as a single stanza, its structure and rime suggest strongly that it is actually two quatrains in common measure, the first with perfect rime (*flower-power*), the second imperfect (*unmoved-God*). Again we see Miss Dickinson's love of alliteration, the organization of meanings about a few key words associated by repeated initial consonant sounds (*f*lower-*f*rost, *b*eheads-*b*lond, *p*lay-*p*ower-*p*asses-*p*roceeds).

Death Is Like the Insect (1716)

Entitled "Death" by its first editors (*Poems,* 1896), this lyric, like #1624, tempts us to interpret it as a parable: perhaps the justification for such a reading is stronger here, since Emily Dickinson casts the whole as a complex simile: "Death is *like.* . . ." The basic image is that of a destructive insect (death) infesting a tree; it will eventually kill it, though it can perhaps be "decoyed" temporarily. So death has a sure hold on every human being, though his coming can sometimes be put off. *Balsam* is a striking term here, for it suggests both the resin from which medicines are made and the tree from which it comes. Saws are used in the amputation of both human and vegetative limbs. But it is worth any sacrifice (even amputation?) to save the life. And if there is no hope, then *wring* the tree (*ring* may be meant, though the anguish of the soul wrung with grief may also be implied), give it up—there is no escaping that insect.

The metric pattern of the stanzas is basically that of common measure, though all unaccented syllables are lost at the starts of lines as are the accented syllables at the ends of the odd-numbered lines. Ironically, there is almost a monotonous sing-song in the rhythm, as though the whole process were a child's game indulged in for sport. The rimes are perfect (likely even those of the second stanza, considering the New England pronunciation: *tree-be, saw-are, skill-will*).

There are numerous examples of alliteration (competent-kill-cost, death-decoyed, bait-balsam-baffle-burrowed, seek-saw-skill).

My Life Closed Twice Before Its Close (1732)

Entitled "Parting" by its first editors (*Poems,* 1896), the lyric is an exaggerated evocation of the anguish of parting (perhaps not so exaggerated, however, if death is meant). The lyric starts with a paradox: the poet's life has "closed" twice before its final close (death); twice she has suffered so devastating an experience that life seemed to end for her (perhaps she is talking of the deaths, say, of Ben Newton and her father—the lyric has not been dated precisely). In fact, the poet wonders whether that final close (death—immortality) may not be an anti-climax after what she has endured in these two earlier experiences. She concludes with a somewhat enigmatic, yet all-revealing paradox: parting is heaven, parting is hell. Perhaps her meaning is that the nearest we come to seeing heaven or to comprehending it in our mortal lives is in those moments of parting with the dying who depart into that realm. But, at the same time, parting is so trying, so difficult, it is very like hell.

The stanzaic pattern is that of common measure, the rimes both perfect (*see-me, befell hell*). There are intricate balancings of thought as well as of syntax and sound (e.g., *twice before—twice befell, so huge—so hopeless, all we know of heaven—all we need of hell*).

Elysium Is as Far as To (1760)

Entitled "Suspense" by its first editors (*Poems,* 1890), the lyric describes the suspense of the soul about to be confronted by one heard coming. The open door can reveal a heaven (Elysium, felicity) or hell (doom), depending upon whose footstep it is. The soul is suspended in a moment of awkward anticipation until it knows who its visitor is (of course, the lyric exaggerates the soul's "fortitude" for a hyperbolic artistic effect: what we have is something like the lady and the tiger situation). (Note that there should be some mark of punctuation after *await* to show that *felicity* is in apposition with *Elysium* and that *doom* introduces the opposite possibility.)

The stanzaic pattern of this brief lyric is common measure, the rimes of the first stanza perfect (*room-doom*), those of the second imperfect (*endure-door*; note how these rimes both echo *doom* in the previous stanza). Note the effects of the contrasts in stanza one (*far-nearest; felicity-doom*), along with the uses of alliteration (*far-friend-felicity-fortitude-foot, doom-door, contains-can-coming*) and consonance (*is-as-as*, far-very-nearest-room-friend, *contains-can-endure-accent-opening*).

Selected Bibliography

Of the making of books about Emily Dickinson there is no end. Publishers are continually announcing new and promising titles. I have selected here only a few of them, particularly those now standard in any Dickinson bibliography.

George Frisbie Whicher's *This Was a Poet: Emily Dickinson* (Ann Arbor, Michigan, 1938), while one of the oldest, is still one of the best accounts of the poet's life and labors. Whicher was among the first to distinguish myth from plausible reality in the biographical and critical history of the poet. He took a sane approach, sorting among the inevitable legends and exaggerations for the truth. Still a masterwork on the poet.

Millicent Todd Bingham's *Ancestors' Brocades* (New York, 1945) and *Emily Dickinson's Home* (New York, 1955) are, respectively, accounts of (1) the preparation of her lyrics and correspondence for publication and (2) her early growth and development, her family, as well as the backgrounds of life in Amherst. Both rely heavily upon the letters and give us our fullest early publication of many of them (of course, that aspect of their usefulness is now superseded by Johnson's three-volume *Letters of Emily Dickinson*). Easy-to-read, fascinating contribution to the Dickinson bibliography.

Richard Chase's *Emily Dickinson* (New York, 1951) is both a biography and a critical commentary. Mr. Chase constructs convincingly the poet's early years and the decades of her poetic development, turning then to formulate her *ars poetica,* the character of her literary contribution. It stands as *The American Men of Letters Series* introduction to her life and work.

Thomas H. Johnson's *Emily Dickinson: an Interpretive Biography* (Cambridge, Massachusetts, 1955) is a succinct and scholarly record of the life and interests of Emily Dickinson. With a remarkable skill and compelling sympathy, Mr. Johnson reveals the forces of family and friends, the psychological and emotional motivations which gave us the poet. His discussions of three major themes (nature, death, and immortality) are masterfully executed. Surely one of the outstanding books on the poet's life and labors.

Theodora Ward's *The Capsule of the Mind: Chapters in the Life of Emily Dickinson* (Cambridge, Massachusetts, 1961) is not only a skillful record of three particular periods in the poet's life (youth, the period of crisis, the last score of years); it also gives an account of her relationship with Mr. and Mrs. Holland (Mrs. Ward's grandparents), Samuel Bowles, and T. W. Higginson. Mrs. Ward's close association with T. H. Johnson in the preparations of the definitive editions of the poems and letters, as well as her own editing of Emily Dickinson's letters to her grandparents, have given her advantages which lend her book authority.

Richard B. Sewell's *Emily Dickinson: a Collection of Critical Essays* (Englewood Cliffs, New Jersey, 1963) brings together commentaries on Dickinson poems by such outstanding critics as Conrad Aiken, Allen Tate, Yvor Winters, George F. Whicher, Thomas H. Johnson, R. P. Blackmur, John Crowe Ransom, Austin Warren, Richard Wilbur, and Archibald MacLeish. A fine introductory collection.

Clark Griffith's *The Long Shadow* (Princeton, New Jersey, 1964) is one of the finest recent studies of Emily Dickinson's poetry itself, focussing upon the tragic themes of her lyrics, in particular treating the "ironical mask" of the poet. Mr. Griffith sees Emily Dickinson as a poet with romantic connections, one with a consistent vision of life, her gaze fixed upon recurring themes (dread, love, death, etc.), her poetic design of limited and consistent range. His explications of individual lyrics are well worth the reading.

S. P. Rosenbaum's *A Concordance to the Poems of Emily Dickinson* (Ithaca, New York, 1964) is an invaluable aid for the serious student of Emily Dickinson's poetry. With the help of such a tool, one may, beyond the basic use of finding a specific passage, make comparisons of vocabulary as used in various lyrics, even discover recurring preoccupations.

* * * *

Among the scores of other titles, these are recommended:

Anderson, Charles R. *Emily Dickinson's Poetry: the Stairway of Surprise*. New York, 1960.

Bianchi, Martha Dickinson. *Emily Dickinson Face to Face*. Cambridge, Massachusetts, 1930.

Capps, Jack L. *Emily Dickinson's Reading*. Cambridge, Massachusetts, 1966.

Higgins, David. *Portrait of Emily Dickinson*. New Brunswick, New Jersey, 1967.

Leyda, Jay. *The Years and Hours of Emily Dickinson*. New Haven, Connecticut, 1960.

Patterson, Rebecca. *The Riddle of Emily Dickinson*. Boston, 1951.

Pollitt, Josephine. *Emily Dickinson: the Human Background of Her Poetry*. New York, 1930.

Porter, David T. *The Art of Emily Dickinson's Poetry*. Cambridge, Massachusetts, 1966.

Taggard, Genevieve. *The Life and Mind of Emily Dickinson*. New York, 1930.

Three Views (Essays by Louise Bogan, Richard Wilbur, and Archibald MacLeish). Amherst, Massachusetts, 1960.

Wells, Henry W. *Introduction to Emily Dickinson*. Chicago, 1947.

Index of
Lyrics Analyzed

The numbers appearing in parentheses after the first-line titles are those assigned the lyrics by Thomas H. Johnson in *Poems of Emily Dickinson* (Cambridge, Massachusetts, 1955). The other numbers identify the pages in this text where analyses of the lyrics may be found.